THE CLIMB

CREATING AN EVEREST MINDSET

RACHEL DAVIS

The Climb
Copyright © 2025 Rachel Davis

Cover design & Interior design by Michael Beas.

Paperback ISBN: 978-1-962825-59-7

FOREWORD

Who would embark on a journey from Lukla Nepal elevation 9,300 feet for a multi-day hike across rugged terrain to the Mount Everest Base Camp at 17,600 feet simply to ensure her 67-year-old father doesn't face such a challenge alone?

Rachel Davis does!!

She has a giver's heart – from working at AmeriCorps Vista helping the Flathead Indian Tribe in Montana, to her service as an Officer in the U.S. Army, to her work with Veteran Support Organizations, to starting a real estate company with the purpose of creating better lives for folks who are struggling.

Rachel is competitive, but she isn't a competitor. She pushes herself to excel but revels in the success of others just as much.

At first glance, she may seem like a naive dreamer. She is! Yet, beneath that exterior lies a determined adventurer, living life as a quest to improve herself, those around her, and the world.

As you journey through this book with Rachel, you'll uncover wisdom and actionable insights that illuminate life as an ongoing adventure.

Who is this book for? While it may not be for everyone, it holds potential for anyone:

- Those who need to create their own crucible
- Individuals transitioning from military to civilian life
- Anyone on their own quest for Everest

Filled with hands-on leadership and life lessons, Rachel shares mindset shifts and emphasizes the foundational role of self-leadership before guiding others.

For anyone contemplating the trek to Mount Everest, this is not merely a narrative but a guide, rich with preparation essentials. Whether redeploying four thousand Soldiers from Afghanistan to the United States or trekking through the Himalayas, preparation remains key. Allow this book to guide you!

This book certainly hits the three E's when I seek something to read: Easy to read, Educational, and Entertaining.

Well done, my friend!

Scott C. Schroeder

For more than a century, Mount Everest has called to the ambitious, the bold, and the broken. Standing at 29,032 feet above sea level, its summit pierces the heavens like a crown of stone and snow. It has been a symbol of triumph, obsession, and all too often, *tragedy*.

Since Sir Edmund Hillary and Tenzing Norgay first stood atop its summit in 1953, thousands have followed in their footsteps, each one chasing a dream carved from ice and ambition. "Because it's there," Hillary famously said when asked why anyone would attempt such a dangerous ascent. A simple answer to an impossible question. That phrase, etched into the lore of high-altitude exploration, has echoed ever since in the minds of climbers, adventurers, and dreamers.

But Everest is not merely a peak to be conquered. It is a graveyard in the sky. More than 300 souls remain on its slopes, entombed forever by the cold. Their bodies, frozen in time, have become grim waypoints on the climb, silent warnings to those who dare ascend. Like Icarus, they soared too close to the sun, tempted by glory, undone by nature.

Despite the risks, hundreds still sign up and line up each season, spending tens of thousands of dollars to endure the thin air, brutal winds, avalanches, and sheer physical toll of the climb. But there's something even more daunting that Everest demands from every soul who dares to approach it, something most people spend their lives avoiding: pain.

That's what makes Everest different. It isn't just altitude or danger. It's the long, slow, burning ache of effort, one that breaks people down to their core long before it ever lifts them up. But pain is something my father and I understand. As Army

Veterans, we have been forged in discomfort. We know what it means to press forward when everything inside you screams _stop_.

That's why, when he looked at me and said, *"Let's take three weeks and go to Everest Base Camp,"* I didn't hesitate.

But the story didn't start there.

Two years earlier, Dad had trekked to Machu Picchu with one of his former platoon leaders—a soldier he once commanded, back when he was a young captain leading troops and carrying the weight of other people's lives on his shoulders. That trip to stirred something in him. It wasn't just nostalgia or adventure— it was purpose. Legacy. A way to reconnect not only with old comrades but with a part of himself that had long been buried under years of sacrifice and structure.

When he came back from Peru, he couldn't stop talking about Everest. Not the summit—he wasn't chasing glory—but Base Camp. The symbolism. The climb toward something with no expectation of flags or fame. He brought it up with friends, one by one. Fellow veterans, neighbors, and even family members. But no one took the bait. Some were too busy. Some were too cautious. Some just weren't wired for altitude or discomfort the way he was.

And then, quietly, he said the words that stopped me cold: *"I think I'm just going to do it alone."*

That was it for me. Absolutely not.

The image of my 67-year-old father—still strong, still stubborn, still leading himself into the unknown—walking into the

Himalayas without anyone by his side lit something fierce in me. I knew he wouldn't ask for company. That's not his style. But I also knew this was more than a trip. This was an adventure in motion. And I wasn't about to let him carry it alone.

I sat down with my husband, Michael, that night and laid it all out—what it would mean, what I'd be walking away from for a few weeks, what I might be walking *into*. We had responsibilities, tight schedules, and a full life. But when I said, *"I can't let him go alone,"* my husband didn't hesitate either.

"Then you need to go," he said.

Because I married a saint. Because he knew—better than I did, maybe—that this wasn't just about Everest. It was about my dad. About healing. About time. And time doesn't wait for the perfect window. It just opens the door—and dares you to walk through it.

I never wanted to conquer Everest.

But I've always wanted to stand in its shadow.

Ever since I was a girl, the lure and mythology of Everest captivated me, not as a peak to be claimed, but as a place where legends walked. I dreamed not of the summit, but of simply being near it. Of feeling the wind and breathing the air that carried so many stories. Of standing where giants once stood, where triumph and tragedy live side-by-side.

I never really believed I'd get there. Life, responsibility, and practicality tend to bury those kinds of dreams as we become employees, spouses, and parents. But in that one unexpected invitation, my father gave me back something I thought I'd lost: the belief that wonder was still possible.

This is the story of that journey. Of altitude and legacy, of fathers and daughters. To the moments when nothing was said, but everything was felt.

It's also the story of healing.

I followed my father into the Army, and walked a path he carved long before I was born.

But we haven't always walked in step. Like many daughters, I grew up trying to understand a man who seemed larger than life, disciplined, driven, and often distant. He was a model soldier, and that kind of excellence demands everything. Unfortunately, there was often little left for home.

My teenage years were tough. I was angry and confused, and he was often gone or mentally preoccupied with the weight of leading others. We collided often; two strong personalities separated by a generation, expectation, and emotion. During my senior year of high school, 9/11 happened, and the world changed. My father deployed to Afghanistan, and the space between us expanded beyond miles.

He was halfway around the world, leading troops in a war I could barely understand, while I was in Seattle, trying to grow up with questions no one seemed to have answers for. The distance wasn't just physical; it was a gap in mindset, in experience, in the way we viewed the world. Our problems didn't speak the same language. His were shaped by life and death. Mine, by confusion and absence. And for a long time, that made me bitter.

I didn't know how to reach him. I wasn't sure I even wanted to. The man I missed felt like a stranger. And in some ways, I let that hurt harden. I held onto it for years.

But time has a way of reshaping our view of things, especially when you carry the weight of the same uniform. After four years in uniform and two deployments to Afghanistan, I decided to leave the service and transition out of active duty.

I began to see just how complicated each Veteran's experience truly is. It's not just medals and memories. It's the quiet recalibration of identity, the invisible bruises no one claps for. It's trying to carry the same discipline into a world that no longer runs on it—and discovering that strength doesn't always translate. I started to understand that service doesn't end. It lingers in the way we walk into rooms, in the things we don't say, in the burdens we don't know how to put down.

What I once saw as indifference in my father, I now recognize as the residue of responsibility. The way a leader learns to compartmentalize, to absorb chaos without complaint. I'm not angry with my dad anymore. I see him more clearly now, not as the man I wished he had been, but as the man he believed he needed to be for our family, and his country. What felt like emotional distance was often just the cost of command. And suddenly, I wasn't just his daughter—I was someone who had stood in the same uniform, under the same flag, with my own shadows trailing behind me.

Veteran stories aren't clean arcs. They're jagged. Layered. And somewhere in that realization, the anger I'd carried for years began to loosen its grip.

Letting go of anger was what made this journey possible. The Everest trek wasn't just a physical challenge, it was a turning point. There was no longer a quiet expectation in me that he should somehow *pay* for the way I felt growing up. That was gone. In its place, there was something softer, stronger: the desire to learn from him. To walk beside him. To take on something hard together, not because we had to, but because we finally could.

He was a month away from turning 68 years old when we took this on. I knew the window for adventures like this wouldn't stay open forever. His body, once forged by rucks, ranges, and years of leading soldiers, was starting to show its age. And yet, here he was, lacing up his boots and flying halfway across the world to walk beside me toward the roof of the world.

I don't know if I'll ever fully find the words to explain what that meant to me. But I felt it in every step. Every mile. Every breath stolen by the thin air of altitude.

This wasn't just about Everest.

This was about us.

TABLE OF CONTENTS

PART

ONE

THE WAR THAT
FOLLOWS YOU HOME

Chapter 1

THE REALITIES OF SERVICE AND SACRIFICE

In 2005, I applied for an Army ROTC scholarship while serving as an AmeriCorps VISTA on the Flathead Indian Reservation in Montana. I had a sociology degree from Washington State University with an emphasis in social work and a drive to make the world better. But purpose doesn't always pay the bills.

AmeriCorps VISTA—Volunteers in Service to America—is a national service program dedicated to fighting poverty through capacity-building work in underserved communities. My role was rooted in service: helping to design programs, write grants, and build local partnerships that could outlast any single volunteer. It was a crash course in resilience, listening before leading, and understanding the systemic nature of hardship. But as much as I loved the mission, I knew I needed something more sustainable—and more structured—to grow into the leader I wanted to become.

That's when I looked to the Army—not just for a paycheck, but for purpose with a plan.

On $800 a month before taxes, I paid $325.12 in rent. (Twelve cents because I lived in apartment #12.) I was broke and idealistic, living on powdered eggs and government cheese. That's when I applied for an Army ROTC (Reserve Officer Training Course) scholarship, it was for stability, not for glory, medals, or adventure.

The following summer, during my first training camp at Fort Knox, Kentucky, I quickly realized I hadn't escaped powdered eggs or government cheese. But something had shifted. The people I met— the grim-faced civilians at Central Issue Facility (CIF) throwing our gear into OD green duffle bags, the fellow cadets getting yelled at by drill sergeants—all became my family. Like any family, we were a mixed bag: funny, flawed, unforgettable.

The Army sparked something in me in my mid-twenties. I had no idea what I wanted to be when I grew up. The Army gave me purpose and direction. It placed me on an azimuth defined in values and the acronym: LDRSHIP—Loyalty, Duty, Respect, Selfless Service, Honor, Integrity, Personal Courage. These weren't abstract. They were drilled into my bones through every ruck march and lesson in leadership.

I learned that challenge is like a muscle, you can train it.

Whether it was crossing a log 30 feet in the air, throwing a grenade, or jumping from a plane—each time, I proved to myself that I could go further by doing hard things. Over time,

I got used to discomfort. I grew stronger, quieter. I got used to being the only woman in the room. And I got used to leading others.

So when I told my friends I was planning to trek to Everest Base Camp with my father, their wide eyes and reactions—words like "incredible" or "insane"—didn't surprise me. I understood their hesitation, but I didn't share it. I'd spent years growing comfortable with challenge. I knew it would push me. I expected it to. But where others saw something nearly impossible, I saw something familiar. The kind of test I was made for. The kind that stirred something deep in me—not fear, but readiness.

But there's another kind of challenge—one that has nothing to do with altitude or endurance. It's the one that waits quietly long after the uniform comes off. The kind that doesn't scream in your face like a drill sergeant, but whispers in the empty spaces of civilian life. It's a fight that is invisible, internal, and unrelenting.

Left unspoken and untreated, those silent battles can claim lives just as surely as any battlefield ever did. The reality of veteran suicide is stark. The "22 a day" number may be debated, but even one is too many. Every day, soldiers lose a battle that doesn't end with war. Behind every statistic is a name, a face, a life. A story interrupted. A heartache that echoes through families and communities. And nearly all of us who served know friends who lost their invisible fight. It hurts on a level that's impossible to describe.

Those of us who come home carry something heavy. The mission ends, but the identity doesn't. The structure disappears, but the discipline lingers. The adrenaline fades, but the awareness never fully does.

For many of us, the hardest part isn't what we faced downrange—it's what we face when we return. The search for meaning when the old mission is gone. That's why purpose matters. That's why challenge still matters. That's why finding your Everest matters.

Out there on the trail with my dad to Everest Base Camp, every step forward meant something. It was about reclaiming that sense of mission. About chasing something higher again— literally and figuratively. Because if you don't find a summit to climb toward, the weight you carry can start to pull you under.

Every Veteran Has an Everest:

For some, that Everest looks like finding a place in a world that doesn't quite know what to do with them. I've seen it firsthand. When I left active duty in 2012, I was an Army Captain with four years of service and two deployments behind me. On paper, I should have been competitive.

During my first deployment, I rerouted an entire brigade's return from Afghanistan amid a civil war in Kyrgyzstan. I was 24 years old. That meant re-planning the movement of thousands of troops, aircraft, and equipment out of a war zone—without access to the air base we had originally been scheduled to use. Overnight, everything changed. I had to find alternate routes through Kuwait and Pakistan, and coordinate complex logistics across multiple countries. There was no playbook. No template. Just pressure and lives depending on it going right.

I didn't panic—I just did what needed to be done. Because that's what soldiers do.

But when I came off active duty and started looking for my next career? Nothing. No callbacks. No interviews. In airports, strangers shook my hand and said, *"Thank you for your service."* In the job market? Crickets.

That's when I realized: *"Thank you for your service"* isn't really about the veteran. It's about the civilian saying it. It makes them feel good. But it doesn't open doors.

In the military, your value is clear. It's worn on your chest, spoken in rank, etched in structure. You earn it through discipline, time, and sacrifice, and everyone knows what it means. But when you step out of uniform, the clarity vanishes. In the civilian world, value is tied to visibility and branding. You must now sell yourself in a language that often isn't yours. And if no one's listening—if no one allows you to translate what you've lived into something they understand—you don't just become overlooked. You are erased. Not because you lack value. But because the world doesn't always know how to *see* it.

That shaped me.

It lit a fire in me that never went out, and never will. Anyone who's worked with me in the Veteran space knows: I don't just advocate—I *go to war* for our people. I fight tooth and nail so Veterans are seen, heard, and hired. Because I *was* that Veteran. The one who couldn't get a callback. The one who was ghosted by companies that couldn't see past the uniform. I know what it's like to be overlooked. And I've made it my personal mission to make damn sure no one else has to go through that alone.

I spent years on the front lines of corporate America, fighting to build real pathways for Veterans—not lip service, not check-the-box initiatives, but systems that *actually worked.* As a subject matter expert in the largest Veteran staffing agency in the United States, I partnered with national companies and government agencies at the enterprise level to design veteran hiring strategies from the ground up. No blueprint. No shortcuts. Our team created an entire vertical where none existed before. And I didn't let companies off easy. I held the mirror up. I pushed them to do better.

Because Veterans bring high-demand skills, knowledge, and abilities into the civilian workplace, and how they are treated in corporate America aren't taglines, they're organizational priorities and *decisions*. You can slap your core values on a glossy brochure and post them on your website, but that's just noise. I don't care what you say in a meeting, I look at where you put your time, your money, your people. That's where your *real* values live. Actions expose priorities. Budgets don't lie. Don't tell me what matters—*show me.*

If a company says it values Veterans but refuses to invest time in understanding their résumés, they don't value Veterans. If they aren't willing to integrate Veterans across leadership and management, especially when those Veterans bring three, ten, sometimes twenty years of transferable experience, they're really not serious. They want the optics, not the outcome.

I've spoken on Veteran transition for years. And here's where I stand: If you say *"thank you,"* you owe a Veteran ten minutes – ask them questions to determine if and where they belong in your organization. If you say hiring them is *"too hard"*, I'm not interested.

All of that; my service, my own struggle to transition, and my years building veteran initiatives, shaped the way I approached the Everest trek. I knew what it meant to carry invisible weight. I knew how disorienting it is to finish one mission and have no idea where the next one begins.

That's why I wasn't intimidated by the trail ahead. I've spent years walking beside people trying to find their next summit. Trying to climb their way back to meaning. Trying to be seen.

So when I laced up my boots for this journey with my dad, it was about reclaiming something.

A shared history. A relationship. A sense of purpose. A test of who we are without the uniform—and what we still carry long after we take it off.

This was our Everest.

And I was ready.

The Importance of Purpose: Mission and Mindset

In uniform, every day has a mission. Whether you are qualifying on the range, prepping for convoy ops, or checking comms before dawn, you know why you are there. Purpose isn't a buzzword, it is your operating system.

And your reason to show up isn't a paycheck.

It is your team. You train with urgency. You serve with intention. You endure because someone else's life depends on your discipline.

And then, one day, it all stops.
No more formation.
No more orders.
No more "why" waiting in your inbox.
The loss of purpose after service isn't a soft landing. It's a free fall.

When the mission ends, the mindset has to carry you.

Because here's the truth: the military doesn't just train skills, it wires mindset.

We're trained to embrace discomfort, not tolerate it, but lean into it, to expect it as part of the path and keep moving anyway. We learn to stay mission-focused under stress, to filter out noise and zero in on what matters most when things get loud, messy, and unpredictable. We're taught how to lead in chaos and uncertainty, how to stand upright when the plan falls apart, and others are looking around for direction.

We're wired to execute without excuses, to make things happen with limited resources, unclear guidance, and impossible timelines. We learn to endure with intention, to suffer with structure, and to keep the team moving, not because it's easy, but because it's necessary. And we build this mindset not through seminars or theory, but through repetition, hardship, and trust.

These aren't motivational phrases.

They're hard-coded principles.

And they don't shut off when the DD-214[1] hits your inbox.

But without a mission to aim at, even the strongest mindset starts to wander. This isn't just a mental health issue, it's a mindset crisis. Because purpose isn't a luxury for Veterans. It's a lifeline.

It's what we're built for. And when it disappears, we don't just get bored, we get lost.
We isolate. We over-adapt. We shrink to fit environments that don't know what to do with our energy. And slowly, that combat-ready mindset, disciplined, focused, resilient, gets buried under routine and disconnection.

---

[1] The DD-214, or *Certificate of Release or Discharge from Active Duty*, is an official document issued to service members upon separation from the U.S. military. It summarizes a Veteran's service, including dates of duty, awards, rank, and discharge status, and is often required to access VA benefits, employment, or educational programs.

But here's the thing:

Veterans don't stop serving. We just need a new direction. According to the National Alliance on Mental Illness, we're 12% more likely to vote and 5% more likely to volunteer than our civilian peers. That's not an accident. That's instinct. We're wired to contribute. To lead. To build. To protect.

Veterans are more likely to be entrepreneurs. We start businesses at higher rates and hire other Veterans when we do. We show up to work earlier. Stay later. We're more likely to pursue advanced training, take initiative, and stay calm under pressure when others fold. We've operated under stress that most people will never understand or face, and we bring that clarity, discipline, and resilience into every boardroom, job site, and team we join. Veterans outperform their civilian counterparts in leadership, problem-solving, and teamwork, especially in complex or high-stakes environments.

We don't shy away from accountability. We *run toward it.* Because for us, service doesn't end at separation, it just shifts form.

But the civilian world doesn't always know how to receive that.

We don't just take off the uniform, we leave behind a warfighting community that *knew us.* We step out of a world where clarity meant life or death and into one where no one says what they mean and everyone's worried about tone.

We're told to soften. To smile. To adapt. But what no one tells us is that we'll lose more than structure, we'll lose *belonging.*

The mission didn't just give us a job. It gave us purpose. It gave us a *name* in the world. It gave us brothers and sisters who would bleed beside us. When that falls away, it doesn't feel like transition; it feels like grief.

And we carry it silently.

That's why mindset isn't just important, it's *everything*. Because when the roles change, when the title no longer defines you, when the structure you've relied on disappears, what's left?

You.

Your beliefs.
Your patterns.
Your ability to stand steady when the ground underneath you shifts.

If you don't have something solid inside, the world will hand you a version of yourself that's smaller than you're meant to be. And you'll start to accept it. Not all at once. Slowly. Quietly. In the way you lower your standards. In the way you hesitate to speak up. In the way you stop showing up fully, even though something inside you is still burning.

That's the danger. Because without a grounded mindset, life doesn't just challenge you, it consumes you.

Mindset is the filter through which you experience *everything*. Your relationships. Your work. Your health. Your decisions. Your leadership. Your capacity to love, to forgive, to rebuild. When your mindset is reactive, fear-driven, or borrowed from someone else, you chase validation instead of purpose. You become a passenger in your own life.

But when your mindset is aligned, intentional, and unshakable, you stop waiting to be chosen. You stop asking for permission. You stop folding every time life applies pressure. Instead, you rise. You adapt. You *decide.* Because mindset isn't just how you think—it's how you *live.*

It's the architectural blueprint of your identity. And if you don't build it with intention, the world will build it for you.

Mindset is the anchor.
Without it, you drift.

MINDSET CHECK
What Do You Hold Onto When the Mission Lets Go of You?

When the mission is clear, everything has weight. Every action matters. Every day starts with purpose. But when that mission ends, the formation is gone, and the identity you've lived by no longer applies, you're not just navigating transition. You're surviving *detachment*.

That's where mindset steps in, not as motivation, but as *oxygen*.

Because without a mission to point your energy at, even the strongest mindset can start to drift. Not from lack of skill, but from lack of *direction*.

And that's the difference between showing up and *still knowing why*.

Ask yourself:

- What part of my identity was shaped by the mission, and what part needs redefining now?
- Am I carrying discipline into this chapter of my life, or just the weight of expectation?
- Where have I been trying to "fit in" instead of *leading forward?*
- What false belief is holding me back from showing up fully in this new space?
- What's one way I can use my mindset, not just to survive this transition, but to *own it?*

Check your mindset. When the mission ends, the *mindset must carry you.* Not just to what's next, but to who you're becoming.

Acclimating to Civilian Life: The Real Climb

Veteran transition is a trek. Not a clean handoff from one life to the next. It's a long, uneven path that forces you to climb through uncertainty, carry weight you can't always explain, and keep moving through moments when the lines on the map are unreadable. For some, the transition out of uniform is full of possibility. For others, it's filled with questions they weren't prepared to ask, about identity, value, direction, and whether the skills they honed in the military still have a place in the world they've returned to.

That's why Everest Base Camp became more than a destination for me. It became a metaphor, a physical expression of what transition actually feels like. The climb was difficult. The altitude affected everything. Some days felt strong and steady. Other days, I was gasping for air. But every step required committed to the goal. Every stretch demanded patience. And I realized, through the rhythm of that trail, that this is exactly what the post-military journey looks like. There are no shortcuts to acclimating. There is no fast-forward through the discomfort. You don't get to skip the hard parts. You have to learn how to breathe again at a different altitude.

Transition is not about chasing a title or rushing toward a civilian version of a "summit." It's about reclaiming your pace. It's about adjusting to new terrain and deciding what kind of leader you're going to be without the rank, the routine, and the uniform. It's about learning to trust your instincts again and knowing that you can lead even when no one is watching. It's about becoming mission-oriented again, but on your own terms.

Veterans need purpose. They need to know that the things they mastered in uniform, the discipline, the grit, the clarity under pressure, still matter. They need to know that their stories, their scars, and their leadership still have weight in rooms that may no longer speak the same language. Purpose is not a "nice to have" in the life of a Veteran; it's a stabilizer. A compass.

The power of the Veteran community lies in its potential to lead, not just in uniform, but in *every space that follows*. That's the heart of this metaphor. The trek wasn't just about reaching Base Camp, it was about what I uncovered along the way: that the leadership we carry, the mindset we've earned, and the sense of mission that shaped us don't disappear when the uniform comes off. They evolve. And they're still *desperately* needed.

But here's the hard truth we're not talking about enough: *fewer and fewer Americans are making the decision to serve.* And when fewer people serve, fewer people even know someone who has. Think about it. I'm 41 years old. Nearly every friend I have grew up with a grandfather who served in WWII. That was normal. That was foundational. That generation wore their service with honor, never seeking the spotlight, and their values bled into the families they raised.

Now ask yourself: how many people do you know who served in Vietnam? Fewer, right? And for millennials, how many of them can name a single peer who deployed to Iraq or Afghanistan? In more and more communities, the answer is very few or *none.*

That's not just a statistic. That's a cultural fracture.

If the Department of Defense continues to miss its recruiting goals, the next generation may grow up with no *living connection* to what it means to serve.[2] No reference point for courage under pressure. No stories passed down about duty, resilience, and the kind of leadership that doesn't flinch when things get hard.

And if our children grow up in a world where service is foreign, how do we expect them to understand its value? How do we expect them to carry the lessons?

Because this isn't just about national defense. It's about national *character.*

Veterans carry more than memories. We carry *muscle memory* for leadership, for urgency, for presence under pressure. We carry the ability to walk into chaos and bring order. To operate in uncertainty without losing clarity. To make decisions when the stakes are high and the margin for error is zero. We carry stories that were never posted, sacrifices no one saw, and a level of accountability that doesn't turn off just because the mission ends.

---

[2]According to Pew Research Center. *The Changing Face of America's Veteran Population.* November 2023: Recent research from the U.S. Department of Defense and Pew Research Center indicates that fewer than 1% of American adults currently serve in the military, down significantly from peak draft-era service in the late 1960s. Projections show the total number of living veterans will decline from 18.3 million in 2023 to approximately 12.1 million by 2048, due to aging populations and lower recruitment rates. Analysts have also noted a growing concentration of military service within legacy families, raising concerns about future civil-military disconnects and the long-term viability of the all-volunteer force.

We carry the scars, physical and invisible, and still show up. We carry the discipline to keep moving when it hurts, and the instinct to serve even when no one's watching. We bring teams together. We stay calm under pressure. We execute when others hesitate. Not because we think we're heroes, but because we've trained too long and too hard to back down when it counts.

We don't just need to thank Veterans — we need to follow them. Into boardrooms. Classrooms. Nonprofits. Innovation labs. Communities.

The mission may change, but the *calling* doesn't.

And if we build systems that recognize that, if we create real pathways for Veterans to lead in every sector, we won't just preserve the best of what military service has given us.

We'll pass it on.

A Different Kind of Isolation:
Leading as a Woman in Uniform

As a woman in the 82nd Airborne, I didn't need anyone to tell me I didn't fully belong. I could feel it in the silence. In the group texts I wasn't on. In the casual conversations I was left out of, not because I wasn't capable, but because I was inconvenient.

I carried the same weight. Met the same standards. Jumped from the same aircraft into the same darkness. But some things, the bonds of camaraderie, the easy trust, and the shoulder claps after long days, were held back from me.

I was treated like a variable to manage. A complication. A risk. Not because of my performance. But because of my presence.

Some of my peers kept their distance, not out of disrespect, but perhaps out of fear of how things "looked", or out of fear of upsetting the perception that I didn't belong. Some might have feared the women back home, wives and girlfriends, who saw my presence as a threat. Therefore, they played it safe and shut me out.

And in the military, where perception is reality, that kind of isolation doesn't stay subtle. It becomes structural. You're not excluded by policy, you're excluded by culture. You're left off emails. Skipped over for informal planning sessions. *You're not in the room when the bond is built*. And by the time the decisions are made, you're too far outside the circle to catch up.

Therefore, you learn to adjust. You learn to walk a narrow line, present enough to lead, quiet enough not to disrupt the illusion of cohesion. You modulate your tone. You double-check your posture. You run every move through a second filter.

And the mindset? It adapts too, but not always in healthy ways.

I armored up. Not out of ego, but out of necessity. I convinced myself I didn't need connection; that being respected was enough. And I could outrun the isolation if I just worked hard enough.

But the truth? That mindset was a survival tool, not a sustainable strategy. I wasn't thriving, I was hardening. I wasn't asking for help, not because I didn't need it, but because I couldn't afford to be seen as needing anything at all.

The military made me mentally tough. But toughness without trust becomes a prison. And strength without support eventually cracks.

And this isn't just a military problem, it's a societal one. We raise girls, telling them they can do anything. We push women to lead, to succeed, to step into rooms they were never expected to be in. And when they get there, we burden them with the silent pressure to be exceptional but not intimidating. We're told we can have it all, but then we are judged when we look tired from carrying the weight of it "all" on our backs.

There's nothing empowering about being overextended and alone. Yet, we keep showing up.

Because women in male-dominated spaces know the truth: You don't just work twice as hard to get half as far. You carry the added weight of constantly proving that you belong there in the first place.

That's why exclusion hits differently. That's why silence from your peers cuts deeper than critique from your subordinates. Because the ones who should have your back are too often afraid of what it might cost them to stand beside you.

Not all of them. Some made space. Some made sure I knew I was seen, not as a woman trying to lead, but as a leader. Period. I'll never forget them. And I'll always be grateful.

When I transitioned out of the military, that ache came with me. Because the bonds I had built,the ones formed in trust and friction, didn't follow me home. Out here, there are no rank structures. No formations. No shared missions.

Civilian life doesn't offer the same camaraderie or the same urgency. And often, it doesn't know what to do with a woman who has been trained to lead under fire and has learned not to flinch.

So you start over. You carry the experience. You carry the weight. And too often, you carry it alone.

That's why mission-aligned, community-driven organizations matter. They don't just help veterans find work. They help you find *your footing again*. They don't treat you like a demographic, they treat you like a leader in transition. They speak the language of service. They understand what mindset you've had to carry, and what it's cost you to keep it intact.

This journey after service isn't just about reintegration, it's about reclamation. It's about reclaiming your voice without shrinking it. Your mission without apology. Your strength without permission. And your space, fully, completely, without compromise.

We weren't built just to survive.
We were built to lead.
And the world needs what we carry.

Mindset Check: Leading Without Belonging

There's a particular kind of weight that comes with leading from the margins.

When you're trusted to carry responsibility, but not fully welcomed into the room.
When you're praised for your strength, but quietly questioned for your presence.
When you're showing up, delivering, and leading, and still wondering if you're being *tolerated* more than *trusted.*

That's where the mindset has to do more than hold you together. It has to *keep you anchored.*

Because navigating leadership without true belonging isn't just exhausting. It's disorienting. And if you're not careful, you start molding yourself to meet expectations that were never made for you. You adapt. You overachieve. You minimize. You endure.

And over time, you start mistaking survival for success.

For those who lead from the margins, ask yourself:

- Am I leading from identity—or performing for acceptance?
- Have I adapted so much that I've lost parts of myself along the way?
- Do I shrink my presence to protect the comfort of others?
- What invisible weight am I carrying just to keep the peace?
- Have I confused resilience with belonging?

For those in the room who've always felt welcomed, ask yourself:

- Who's missing from the table—and why?
- When was the last time I yielded space, not just shared it?
- Do I listen to understand—or to respond?
- Am I mistaking someone's quiet endurance for contentment?
- When someone challenges the norm, do I get curious— or get defensive?

Check your mindset.
Leadership without belonging will harden you.
Leadership with belonging will *liberate* you.
You don't have to trade authenticity for access
And you don't have to do it alone.

PART

TWO

THE ROAD TO THE MOUNTAINS

Mindset Shift: Answering the Call – This journey wasn't about proving my strength. It was about choosing connection over comfort and showing up with purpose.

A Legacy of Grit

My father and I aren't wired to slow down. Maybe it's the years of service that include decades of early mornings, structured chaos, and a mindset tuned to urgency. Or, maybe it's something older, passed down like muscle memory. A quiet defiance of time. A refusal to let age dictate purpose. Whatever it is, it runs deep in us. It includes an internal drive, a restlessness, and that instinct to keep going.

He's always led from the front. He had all the Army badges to prove it: Ranger School, Airborne School, Air Assault School and the chest of medals to indicate a lifetime in the Infantry. But he didn't just wear the tab, wings and medals. He lived the values behind them. When I earned my own wings in 2009, he pinned his onto my chest with the 34-foot towers in the background. It's one of my favorite photos of the two of us. It wasn't just a rite of passage, it was a transfer of legacy. A tangible moment where bloodline met mission. Later in 2009 we even deployed at the same time. I went to Afghanistan, and he went to Iraq. And when I was promoted to First Lieutenant in 2010, he did it across two war zones, his voice cutting through the Video Teleconference Capability (VTC) feed to read the orders promoting me with a whole lot of pride, in the small Tactical Operations Center (TOC). No big ceremony. Just two Soldiers connected by blood and belief.

But our family's connection to service didn't start or end with us. It's become something of a family business. I possess a black powder rifle from an ancestor who fought in the Civil War. (His initials are carved into the stock, "JTA" for John Tyler Arnet.)

My grandfather served in both the Navy and the Coast Guard, surviving a ship nearly sinking that was cut in half by another ship. That kind of resolve lives beyond the page. It lives in your DNA. And even though I come from a small family, just two cousins, both male, both living in Portland, Oregon, the military legacy somehow found its way to me.

And here's the thing: My grandfather was proud. Deeply proud. He never said it outright, not in those words, but you could see it in his eyes. I think it confused him a little, honestly. That it was me, his granddaughter, who wore the uniform during a time of war, not the two grandsons who lived closer. There was a generational divide there, but it didn't break the bond. If anything, it strengthened it.

Even when dementia began to chip away at his memory, he never forgot that I served. During visits to his memory care facility, his eyes would light up when he saw me. He'd tell anyone within earshot, staff, other residents, strangers in the hallway, "That's my granddaughter. She's in the Army." His pride was radiant, like a lighthouse cutting through the fog of what his mind no longer held onto. He didn't remember the details of my job. He didn't need to. He remembered that I served. And in those moments, we were still connected, uniform to uniform, generation to generation.

And then there's my father.

Retirement didn't slow my father down, either. If anything, it amplified who he already was. He got stronger, sharper, more disciplined. He didn't chase youth, he chased growth. His mindset didn't retire. His work ethic didn't soften. On the trek, he moved with focus and presence. He led without words.

Every morning, he rose with quiet intention, and reflected and practiced gratitude. This was the same man who once told me in a counseling session, flat out, "I have no emotional needs." And here he was, standing in the Himalayas, talking about mindset and presence like a Buddhist monk in trekking boots.

That was the real evolution. Not in his gear or gait, but in his willingness to grow. To stay in the climb, not toward glory, but toward understanding. To stay open. To lead with presence instead of pressure. The grit was still there, but now it was deeper. More refined. Less about proving and more about becoming.

This trek didn't just bring us closer. It showed me something about the kind of leader I want to be, not just in moments of adrenaline or intensity, but in the stillness. In the reflection. In the quiet strength of consistency.

This wasn't just a hike. It wasn't even just a pilgrimage to Everest Base Camp. It was a return, to connection, to lineage, and to the unshakable truth that leadership doesn't expire with age or fade after service. It matures. It listens more than it speaks.

What I carry forward isn't just my father's discipline or my grandfather's pride. I carry the understanding that what sustains us is always shifting. It's not about how hard you can push. It's about how deep you can reach when you're stripped of ego. How much you can evolve without letting go of your foundation. And how many people you can lift, not just by being strong, but by being present.

That's not just resilience or tradition. In my family, it is bigger than legacy, it has become a birthright.

MINDSET CHECK
Legacy in Motion

Legacy isn't a finish line. And it's not what people write in a speech after you're gone.
It's the day-to-day impact of how you show up. How you lead.

This isn't just about where you've been, it's about who you're *becoming*. And whether the strength you carry forward is rigid out of habit, or refined by growth.

Because sometimes, the hardest thing to do isn't holding the line. It's letting go of the version of strength that kept you alive, but no longer helps you evolve.

Ask yourself:

- Am I clinging to the version of strength I was taught, or am I open to evolving it?
- What legacy am I living, and what legacy am I *building*?
- Who came before me that shaped my mindset? Who do I want to influence after me?
- Do I equate growth with grinding, or do I give myself space to reflect and expand?
- Have I confused resilience with silence? Have I armored up at the expense of connection?

Check your mindset.
Legacy isn't built in the spotlight. It's forged in the quiet, daily decisions of how you lead —with courage, clarity, and *intention.*

THREE

THE CLIMB TO BASE CAMP
CAMP
– A DAY BY DAY ACCOUNT

Chapter 1

THE TRAVEL AND LANDING IN KATHMANDU

The journey began not with a step, but with a series of takeoffs. Charlotte to Atlanta. Atlanta to Istanbul. Istanbul to Kathmandu. It took two full days, but truth be told, we slept surprisingly well. My father had booked us lay-flat seats for the long hauls, and I'd never experienced that kind of comfort in the air before. I stretched out under a blanket, watched a few movies, ate my weight in warm rolls, and drifted into real sleep somewhere over the Atlantic. My poor husband now knows I've discovered a new standard for international flights, and I'm not going back.

By the time we landed in Nepal, we were well-rested and wide-eyed.

The moment those airport doors slid open, we were hit with it: the sounds, the smells, the dust, the colors, the chaos. It was as if Kathmandu had been waiting behind a curtain, ready to pull us in. Our driver found us quickly, waving a small sign with our names scribbled across it. He greeted us with a wide smile and a firm handshake, then leaned in with a quick word of advice: *"Don't give money to anyone. If someone says they're with us, just ignore them."*

I nodded, and tried to play it cool. But within ten minutes, a bit foggy from travel, still trying to figure out if my feet were on solid ground, I handed a stranger $20. I honestly couldn't tell you why. He stepped forward confidently, reached for a bag, and in my haze, I assumed he was part of the team. He took the cash, smiled, and disappeared into the crowd. I turned to see our actual driver watching me with a look that said *I literally just told you not to do that.* Lesson learned.

From that point on, it felt like stepping into a world where the ancient and the unfamiliar collided —where timeless rituals met my modern confusion, and every step carried the weight of both wonder and dissonance.

Kathmandu is unlike anywhere I've ever been. Urban sprawl there isn't just expansive —it's vertical, chaotic, alive. The city looks like it's been poured into a bowl and kept growing in every direction. Buildings lean on one another like tired hikers. Rooftops turn into terraces, terraces into half-finished construction zones, with rebar sticking out like radio antennas waiting for a signal from the future.

We weaved through the maze of the city in a way that felt more like survival than navigation. Cars, buses, motorcycles, everything moves at once, and somehow doesn't collide. We drove on the left side of the road, but it quickly became clear that lanes were just suggestions. Motorcycles buzzed by like angry bees, weaving between trucks and people. No one was going fast, but everything felt like it might crash at any second. It was a kind of mechanical ballet, messy, loud, and impossibly graceful.

We passed the King's Palace, now a museum, a shell of royalty in a nation that shed its monarchy in 2008. Nepal is still young as a democracy, shaped by a violent history of Maoist rebellion and political upheaval. And yet, for all its past, the energy of Kathmandu wasn't heavy. It felt forward-moving. Determined. Unapologetically alive.

And that's what made my heart ache.

Because I'd seen another version of this story play out in Afghanistan. I'd flown over cities filled with potential, with people who wanted peace and progress, and watched as it unraveled, undone by power, corruption, extremism, and exhaustion. In Afghanistan, buildings still stood behind barbed wire, guarded by men with rifles and haunted by what could've been. There was no casual walk past a former royal compound. No motorbikes buzzing by in chaotic harmony. No backpackers sipping coffee under prayer flags. Just checkpoints. And eyes that had seen too much.

Nepal reminded me of what I had hoped for. What I had *worked* for. A fragile but growing democracy. A place where people had endured chaos and violence and somehow kept moving forward. It didn't feel like a perfect place, but it felt possible. And I couldn't help but wonder what Afghanistan might look like if the world had chosen differently.

Seeing Nepal like this, a country that had come through its own fire and still chose freedom, it stirred something in me. It made me proud of what we were about to do, but it also made me grieve for what I'd once believed we could help build somewhere else.

Eventually, miraculously, we arrived at the Hotel Thamel Park, tucked just off the heart of Thamel Street. If Kathmandu is a sensory overload, Thamel is its epicenter. A narrow stretch pulsing with trekkers, vendors, music, prayer flags, and the scent of every spice imaginable. Gear shops sell everything from knockoff North Face jackets to genuine mountaineering essentials. Cafes line the road, squeezed between bars, trekking agencies, and stores selling yak wool scarves and singing bowls. Dozens of languages dance in the air. If you're heading to the mountains, this is your launchpad. If you're returning, it's your soft landing.

We checked in, dropped our bags in the room, and finally paused. I could see the fatigue in my father's shoulders, but I could also see something steadier beneath it. A quiet resolve.

Later that evening, we met Dil, the Founder and CEO of Alpine Ramble. He greeted us not like clients, but like old friends. There was something in his presence that was calm, steady, and kind. He was a leader without needing to prove it. He asked us about our journey, how we were feeling, how we'd prepared. And when he looked at my father, I saw something flicker in his eyes. It was respect, maybe even something protective.

"I'm proud of how much you've prepared," he said. And I believed him.

My father never said it out loud, but I knew he carried questions. About his age. About his ability. *Can I really do this?* Dil seemed to understand without needing to ask. He didn't dwell on it. Instead, he outlined the itinerary with quiet confidence, always ending with the same reminder: *"It's flexible. We'll take it day by day. You're family now."*

And somehow, I knew he meant that, too.

That night, we also met Preshant, our guide for the journey. He was younger, calm, and observant. At first, he kept his words brief, letting us settle in. But there was something unspoken between us, a thread I wouldn't fully recognize until much later. Preshant would become my *bhai*, my little brother. And I, his *didi*, his big sister. That bond, like the trail itself, would be built one step at a time.

Dad and I made our way up to the rooftop bar of the hotel that evening, grabbed a couple of beers, and sat quietly as the lights of Kathmandu blinked to life across the valley. The city stretched out below us, lively, chaotic, and beautiful in its own way. We didn't say much, just watched it all unfold in silence, letting the moment settle in.

We crashed early, sometime around 9 p.m., and like clockwork, we both woke up at 3 a.m., a mix of jet lag and that restless energy that comes when you know something big is ahead. We weren't exactly well-rested, but that wasn't new to us. Years in the Army had taught us how to run on fumes when it mattered. Excitement was doing the heavy lifting now. Without needing to say it, we got up, moving quietly, double-checking our gear and packing up for the next step: the flight from Kathmandu to

Lukla. For now, though, we were just two travelers in a dusty, dazzling city, standing on the edge of something far bigger than either of us could yet understand.

MINDSET CHECK
Crossing Thresholds

Every journey begins before the path is visible.
Sometimes it starts at the trailhead.
Or in an airport terminal, a sudden detour, or a decision made in motion.

Before you summit anything, you have to *land somewhere.*
And how you land, how you meet the unfamiliar, matters more than most people realize.

Because the first threshold isn't physical.
It's *mental.*

And if you cross it without awareness, you risk missing the very thing that was meant to shape you.

Ask yourself:

- Do I try to control unfamiliar environments, or let them teach me something new?
- When things don't go as planned, do I default to frustration, or lean into flexibility?
- Am I present enough to notice the beauty in chaos, or too busy rushing to make it make sense?

Check your mindset.
Thresholds aren't always marked by signs or maps.
Sometimes they're internal. And crossing them well means letting go of control long enough to *receive what the moment is offering.*

DAY 1
Kathmandu – Lukla - Phakding

The Everest Base Camp trek begins with an unforgettable flight from Kathmandu to Lukla, which is home to what's widely considered the most dangerous airport in the world.

Our flight left closer to lunchtime, not the early morning departure we had expected. It turned out there had been a miscommunication. Dil, always respectful of people's pace, had thought we wanted a day to explore Kathmandu. But my father and I were ready to go. We didn't come for the city, we came for the mountains. By the time we boarded, we were on the last flight of the day. And while we hadn't realized it then, this kind of flexibility, both from us and from Alpine Ramble, would become a theme throughout the trek.

We flew Sita Air, a small domestic carrier with a fleet of twin-prop planes designed for the tight and volatile weather of the Himalayas. The airport was busy, but not overwhelming. Security was light but present, and after a quick check, we were handed a basic boarding pass, just a piece of paper, no barcode, nothing digital, and directed toward a waiting bus. We rode across the tarmac toward our plane, the Himalayas rising in the distance like ancient sentinels. I would've been overwhelmed if we were on our own. But Prashant, our guide, handled everything, calm, steady, precise. He directed us where to go, when to board, and somehow made the hectic buzz of the domestic terminal feel like a private concierge service.

It was the first moment I realized just how valuable having a guide truly was. Prashant wasn't just helping us on the trail, he was smoothing every edge of the journey. His relationships with the airlines, the lodges, the porters, and even the helicopter companies would show up again and again. This wasn't just a guided trek. It was a network of trust built by Alpine Ramble, and it made a difference every single day.

As we lifted off from Tribhuvan International Airport, I pressed my forehead to the window. The left side of the plane, the *pro tip* if you want the best views. Even through the haze, I could see the Himalayas stretching out in the distance like a row of jagged teeth, growing clearer with every mile. Flying next to them, not above, but beside, felt surreal. These weren't clouds, they were giants.

The flight to Lukla is only 25 minutes, but the last five are unforgettable. As we began our descent, the plane curved and banked tightly through narrow valleys. You can see straight into the cockpit the entire time, every dial, every movement, every breath of the pilots. They're not just trained, they're *certified* specifically for this route. Pilots must undergo extensive high-altitude and short-takeoff-and-landing (STOL) training to be cleared for Lukla. And watching them maneuver through these mountains, it made sense. There's no radar, just experience, visibility, and guts.

Lukla Airport, officially Tenzing-Hillary Airport, is perched at 2,845 meters (9,334 feet). The runway is only 527 meters (1,729 feet) long and slopes upward at a 12% gradient. For comparison, a typical commercial airport runway in the U.S. is over 10,000 feet long—Lukla's is shorter than five football fields laid end to end. One end of it ends in a rock wall. The other, a sheer drop into the valley below. There are no second chances here. Either the pilot lands it cleanly, or they circle back to try again—if the weather allows.

And if the length wasn't intimidating enough, the runway is also just 24 meters (79 feet) wide—narrower than the wingspan of many small aircraft that land there. For reference, a Boeing 737 has a wingspan of over 35 meters. At Lukla, there's no room for error. Gusty crosswinds, unpredictable cloud cover, and shifting visibility make the final descent more art than science.

This isn't just one of the most dangerous airports in the world—it's a runway that tests precision, nerve, and total command of the aircraft. The mountain doesn't offer grace for hesitation. It demands your complete attention.

We were lucky. No turbulence. Clear skies. No delay. And on that last flight of the day, we touched down smoothly onto the slanted runway, to a smattering of applause from the other passengers.

That luck, I would later learn, wasn't guaranteed. My father and I had planned our trip during the Spring shoulder season. In trekking terms, shoulder season refers to the edges of the Everest Base Camp window—those transitional months between the high traffic of peak season and the unpredictability of the off-season. There are two: one in late February to mid-March, and the other in late November into early December. The weather can be colder, especially in the mornings and at altitude, and some teahouses begin to close for winter. But the reward is fewer crowds, clearer skies, and a kind of solitude that transforms the Khumbu[3] into something deeply personal. It's not always the most comfortable time to trek, but for those willing to trade convenience for clear skies, shoulder season offers a raw, reflective version of the Himalayas—less traveled, and in many ways, more revealing.

But early March falls just before that window, when winter is still loosening its grip and conditions can shift by the hour. During this time, flights into Lukla often face delays or cancellations due to sudden fog, wind, or cloud cover. By mid-March, air traffic increases so dramatically that flights from Kathmandu are often rerouted or suspended altogether. Instead, trekkers take bumpy jeep rides for hours to reach a more remote regional airport, where flights to Lukla may still operate—weather permitting.

Even then, it's not uncommon to wait days for a clear landing window. If the pilot can't see the runway, the flight simply won't happen.

But today, we had the sky on our side. Lukla isn't just an airport, it's a rite of passage. The gateway to Everest. The place where the trail truly begins.

As we stepped off the plane and into the thin mountain air, I looked at my father. He was grinning, his boots already pointed toward the trail.

---

[3] *Khumbu* is a region in northeastern Nepal that encompasses the southern slopes of Mount Everest and is home to the famous Everest Base Camp trekking route. It includes villages like Namche Bazaar and Tengboche, and is part of the Sagarmatha National Park, a UNESCO World Heritage Site. The Khumbu is also the ancestral homeland of the Sherpa people, who have lived and guided in the high Himalayas for generations.

We made our way to Khumbu Lodge for lunch, where we met our porter, Robin, for the first time. He was just 17-years-old, with a quiet presence and an easy smile. Prashant pointed him out casually as we sipped tea, and I was immediately struck by two things: his socks were black, with bright orange and yellow flames licking up the sides, and the way he was methodically tying our packs together, preparing to carry nearly 60 pounds of gear up the trail.

Robin was, by all definitions, a mountain boy. He had grown up in a small village more than six hours' walk from Lukla. Not drive. *Walk.* He had been moving through these hills since he could walk, and it showed, not just in his balance or strength, but in the way he moved with the land. He was confident, sure-footed, and patient.

Watching him work, I realized how much I didn't know about what it meant to carry weight in the Himalayas. Robin didn't throw the packs over his shoulders like a backpack. Porters in this region carry their loads with a *namlo*, a thick strap that wraps around the load and is looped across the top of the forehead. The weight is supported by the head and neck, not the back. It's ancient, efficient, and brutally hard. Robin leaned forward slightly, centering the load with practiced efficiency, then tightened the straps and waited, barely breaking a sweat.

He didn't speak much English, and we didn't yet know any Nepali, but it didn't matter. In those early moments, communication wasn't about language, it was about respect. His quiet nods, his readiness, the careful way he made sure our bags were secure. It spoke volumes.

There was no ceremony to his strength. No bravado. Just this unspoken message: *I've got you.*

And he did.

We hadn't even left the village of Lukla before the mountains stopped us in our tracks. Surrounded on all sides, they rose like ancient stone sentinels. They were massive, layered, and endless. Jagged peaks cut into the sky, snow-dusted ridgelines stretched in every direction, and the air felt crisp and impossibly pure. It was hard to imagine that anyone could be in a rush here. Just standing still felt like an act of reverence.

Lukla itself was more like a mountain outpost than a town. It was a hub, one that pulsed with purpose. All supplies for the villages along the trek are flown into Lukla from Kathmandu. From there, they're loaded onto donkeys and yaks that carry everything, rice, propane, tea, toilet paper, even plywood, up and down the trail. There are no roads. No vehicles. Just muscle and endurance.

As we moved through town, I noticed traditional Nepali homes—rectangular stone structures with tin roofs and brightly painted window frames. Many had simple cloth-coverings hanging over the doorways, fluttering softly in the breeze, offering privacy and protection without the need for a door that would only be battered by wind and dust.

Stray dogs wandered the cobbled streets, curling at the feet of resting trekkers. A golden statue of Sir Edmund Hillary and Tenzing Norgay stood at attention. Just beyond it, the Pasang Lhamu Gate, named for the first Nepali woman to summit

Everest, stood tall and unshaken. Carved women holding offerings flanked the archway.

It was a threshold. A crossing over.

And we had just taken our first step.

The trail to Phakding is one of the easier days, about 6 kilometers (3.7 miles), mostly downhill from 2,860 meters (9,383 feet) to 2,610 meters (8,562 feet). It took us just under three hours, winding along the banks of the Dudh Koshi River, which would become a companion over the coming days, always rushing beside us.

Right out of the gate, we encountered our first mani walls—long stacks of carved stones inscribed with ancient Buddhist prayers and mantras, often in Tibetan script. The tradition is to always pass to the left, keeping the inscriptions on your right for good fortune and safe passage. The ritual of it grounded me more than I expected. You're not just walking through nature here. You're walking through faith, culture, and memory.

There were prayer wheels too, metal cylinders set into rows of stone, meant to be spun clockwise as you pass. Each turn sends the engraved mantra "Om Mani Padme Hum"[4] into the universe. I spun them all.

It wasn't long before we came to our first suspension bridge, long, narrow, and strung with a tangle of colorful prayer flags. They flapped in the wind like they were cheering us on. These

---

[4] *Om Mani Padme Hum* is a six-syllable Sanskrit mantra commonly translated as "the jewel is in the lotus." Associated with the Bodhisattva of compassion, Avalokiteśvara, it symbolizes the union of wisdom and compassion in the path to enlightenment.

Buddhist prayer flags are everywhere on the trail, and each color represents an element: blue for sky, white for air, red for fire, green for water, and yellow for earth. They're meant to bless the wind as it passes, spreading goodwill and compassion. You don't tie new ones for yourself, you do it for others. That stuck with me.

We passed donkey trains and yak herds, their bells clanging in rhythmic harmony, echoing off the valley walls. The animals moved with purpose, always led by a handler who barely had to raise his voice. They knew the path.

And then there were the porters.

One man, no more than 100 pounds himself, carried a prayer wheel that easily weighed 200 pounds, strapped to his back and supported by a *namlo*. Every few steps, he'd pause, resting the load on a walking stick, then press on. I felt humbled watching him. Robin, our 17-year-old porter, had already passed us at least once by then, his flame socks flashing as he moved ahead with our packs. Light and steady. Like the mountain was his playground.

Kids played on the side of the trail, waving and calling out, "Namaste!" with their palms pressed together in greeting. Some were barefoot, others bundled in mismatched layers, but every one of them had a smile that cut straight through the dust and distance. "Namaste," we'd echo back, and I'd feel the weight of that word: "I see the divine in you."

Meals along the trail averaged about $4 if you were eating off the economy menu. Most menus featured variations of the same staples: fried rice, noodles, soups, vegetable momos, and dal bhat. My father and I had decided to go vegetarian for the trip. Yaks and donkeys were the only supply chain, and we couldn't be sure how long meat had been out by the time it hit a plate, especially as we climbed higher. Besides, the vegetarian options were delicious and filling.

That night, we stayed in a traditional tea house with stone walls and wooden trim. Our room had two twin beds, an electric blanket (a luxury we'd come to treasure), and an incredible view of the river and a suspension bridge just down the trail. We even had a private bathroom with a Western toilet and a shower, another luxury we knew wouldn't last much longer.

Dinner was dal bhat made from lentils, rice, curried vegetables, and pickles. It's a staple for Nepali people, not just because it's nutritious, but because it's the only meal on the trail that comes with unlimited refills. For mountain people doing hard work, dal bhat is fuel. And for trekkers like us, it was a chance to sit down, warm up, and reflect.

As we settled in for the night, I looked out the window one last time. The river shimmered under the moonlight, and the sound of bells from a passing donkey train echoed in the distance. I didn't know what the trail would ask of me in the days ahead, but I knew something had already shifted.

MINDSET CHECK
The Power of Starting Small

Not every journey begins with a roar.
Sometimes, it starts in a whisper.
A delayed flight. A language barrier. A porter in flame socks
who says more through presence than words.

The truth is, strength doesn't always announce itself.
Progress doesn't always show up on time.
And the beginning of something meaningful often feels like
uncertainty wrapped in inconvenience.

But that's the point: mindset isn't built at the summit, it's
shaped in the first few, fragile steps.

Ask yourself:

- How do I respond when the path changes before I've
  even started?
- Do I recognize support when it shows up quietly, or only
  when it's loud and obvious?
- Am I open to learning from those younger than me,
  quieter than me, or walking beside me unnoticed?
- Do I rush through beginnings, or allow myself to *honor*
  them?
- What small rituals am I missing in my life because I've
  been too focused on the summit?

Check your mindset. Every journey worth taking asks you to
release control before it demands your strength. Starting small
isn't a weakness; it's a *discipline.* It's where presence becomes
power.

Spiritual Wealth, Material Simplicity

That first night in Phakding, lying under a thick quilt with the electric blanket beneath me, I couldn't help but take inventory, not of miles or elevation, but of the shift that was already beginning to take root inside me.

We hadn't even reached 9,000 feet, and yet everything felt different. Slower. Simpler.

In the West, simplicity is often sold as a lifestyle, a curated aesthetic, minimalist furniture, a smaller wardrobe, and a meditation app. But here, in the mountains of Nepal, simplicity isn't a lifestyle. It's life. It's a necessity. There is no excess. No space for clutter. Everything that's here was carried in by someone's hands or the back of an animal. Everything has weight. And because of that, everything has value.

The tea is hot and made to last. The meals aren't fancy, but they are nourishing. The rooms are small. There's no luxury in the traditional sense. But there is kindness. Every smile from a stranger, every "namaste" from a child on the trail, every carved mani stone placed with care, these are signs of abundance. Not material, but spiritual.

I had spent years in places where survival was loud, sharp-edged, and heavy with grief. Where faith often felt weaponized or hidden under layers of fear and loss. In Afghanistan, I saw devotion tested daily. I saw people hold tight to their belief even as their world burned around them. But here in Nepal, the faith I was witnessing felt weightless and woven into daily life. It wasn't proclaimed, it was practiced.

The porters carried not just gear but reverence. Every time a prayer wheel was spun, it was not a show; it was a message. A whisper to the universe. The mani walls, the flags, the memorial stones etched with the names of loved ones lost to the mountains, they weren't just traditions. They were reminders. That we are passing through. That life is brief. It should be walked with intention.

There is immense dignity in that kind of simplicity.

I thought of home, and of schedules and stresses of accumulating things, of striving. I thought of the way we measure wealth: bank accounts, square footage, titles. None of that existed here. And yet, in the quiet, in the mountain air, in a small room overlooking a bridge strung with prayer flags, I felt something deeper than comfort. I felt peace.

It made me wonder what real wealth looks like. Maybe it's not what we store, but what we share. Not what we build, but what we carry for others. Not how much we own, but how often we stop to spin a wheel, whisper a prayer, and give thanks for the trail under our feet.

Out here, stripped of the noise and the grind, I could see it clearly: spiritual wealth isn't about escaping the world. It's about engaging it with open hands and a steady heart.

And maybe, just maybe, that's the kind of wealth that endures.

MINDSET CHECK
Honor the Beginning

The first stretch of the journey rarely feels like a test of strength, but it's almost always a test of *awareness*.

The trail from Lukla to Phakding wasn't hard on the body, but it shifted something deeper. It asked me to slow down. To listen. To notice that the world was moving differently, and that maybe I needed to, too.

I wasn't just shedding altitude. I was shedding instinct. I stopped marching like a soldier and started learning how to move like a *student*. And that shift didn't weaken me. It sharpened me.

Ask yourself:

- Do I treat the beginning of something as blessed, or just something to push through?
- Am I paying attention to who's supporting me quietly, even if they don't speak my language?
- Is my pace driven by ego or alignment?
- When I feel the need to push forward, am I missing what's being offered right where I am?
- Am I willing to redefine what strength, leadership, and progress look like for this season?

Check your mindset.
The incline may not have started yet, but the internal climb has. And if you're not paying attention, you'll miss the moment the real journey begins.

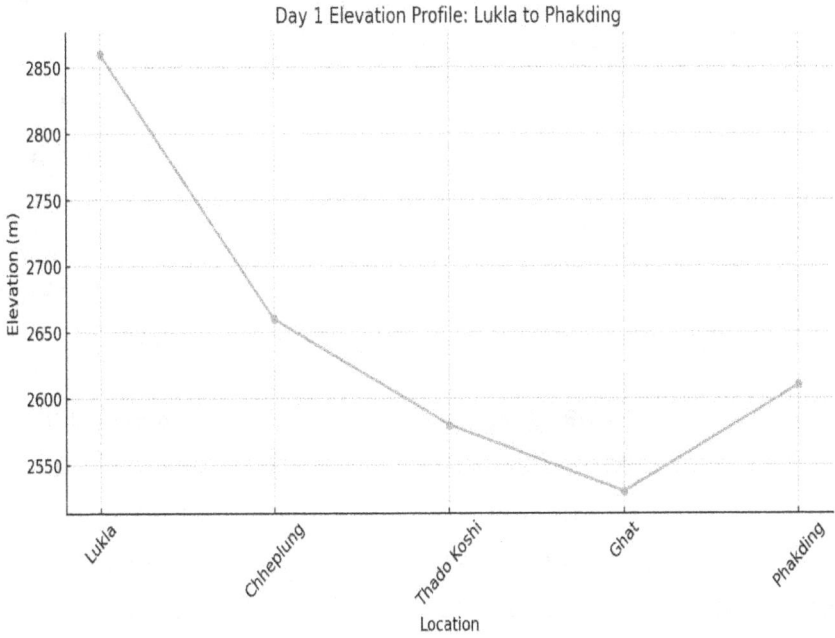

Day 1 Elevation Profile: Lukla to Phakding

DAY 2
Phakding to Namche Bazaar:
When the Trail Demands More

Mindset Shift: From Enduring to Adapting – Leadership means knowing when to ask for help and when to recalibrate.

We awoke to golden light casting long shadows through the pine forest lining the Dudh Koshi River. Ginger lemon tea in hand, my father and I sat quietly on the deck of our tea house, watching the sun crest behind the peaks. There was a silence between us that didn't need to be filled. The peace of that moment gave little warning of how hard the day would be.

The route from Phakding to Namche Bazaar covers just 11 kilometers. On paper, it's a reasonable trek, roughly six hours for most. But what the map doesn't show is the brutal elevation gain: nearly 2,500 feet, all above 8,000 feet of altitude. The terrain rolls up and down constantly, offering no consistent rhythm. It was like climbing a staircase designed by a sadist, with each step heavier than the last.

As we began hiking, I noticed Prashant sipping from a thermos filled with Sherpa tea, a salty, buttery drink made from yak milk and black tea. It's not for everyone, but in this region, it's fuel. The salt helps replenish electrolytes, and the fat offers calories for the cold. I remember thinking how strange it was that something so simple was so necessary up here.

The temperature difference was striking. In the early morning, the cold clung to the valley like a second skin. I hiked in layers, breath fogging in front of me. But once the sun broke through the trees, everything changed. Within minutes, I was sweating under all those clothes. Every step became a negotiation between overheating and freezing.

About midway through the day, we approached the entrance to Sagarmatha National Park, near the village of Monjo. The first thing that caught my eye was the large 3D model of the Everest region, a scale replica mounted under a protective shelter. It was mesmerizing. You could trace the entire route to Base Camp with your finger, watching the trail snake through valleys and over passes, up to the flanks of the highest point on Earth. Seeing the terrain laid out like that, every peak labeled, every glacier marked, gave a deeper perspective to what we were doing. It made the trek feel both more achievable and more intimidating. This wasn't just a hike, it was a journey through giants.

Just beyond the model stood the gateway to the park itself, a beautiful stone archway adorned with Tibetan prayer inscriptions and flanked by prayer wheels that spun with a satisfying thud. The top of the arch read, *"Sagarmatha National Park: A World Heritage Site"*, in both English and Nepali. Walking beneath it felt ceremonial, like crossing a threshold between the ordinary and the ancient.

We signed into the tourist check post, handed over our TIMS card and park permits, and entered the UNESCO-protected region. This land—home to the Sherpa people, elusive snow leopards, ancient monasteries, and the world's tallest peaks, demands respect.

The rivers we followed were milky-white with glacial runoff—meltwater from Everest, Lhotse, and Nuptse that carried ancient ice down through rock and time. You could taste the cold just by looking at them.

Trekking through the park reminded me of coastal Northern California—specifically, the Pacific Coast Highway near Big Sur. The towering pines, the switchbacks, the way the trees framed the light and opened onto sweeping views. But this place was wilder. Harsher.

Porters passed us regularly, carrying burdens that defied belief. Enormous loads strapped to their backs, their balance aided by short, T-shaped walking sticks they'd wedge into the ground to shift weight during rest stops. These sticks weren't for pacing, they were for surviving.

In this space, I was once again the only woman. It wasn't new—but what wasn't said always lingered. Every time I stepped into a group like this, there was an invisible weight that came with being the outlier. Not just carrying your own pack, but the unspoken pressure to keep up, to not be the reason anyone had to slow down.

One of the first and most important lessons on the trek is to set a sustainable pace. Everyone tells you this. The altitude demands patience. But I didn't listen.

I was eager. Eager to prove I could hang. Eager to push myself. Eager to show that I wasn't the weak link. That eagerness, that old instinct to overperform in order to belong, followed me up the trail.

And it would cost me.

Because the mountain doesn't respond to effort the way the world below does. It doesn't reward sheer will or hustle. It demands humility. Demands that you listen—to your breath, your body, the terrain beneath your boots. And when you don't, it has a way of making you.

We stopped for lunch, and I made the mistake of ordering dal bhat. It was too heavy. I didn't know it yet, but my hydration levels were already crashing. I chalked up the sluggishness I felt to the side effects of Diamox.

About 30 minutes after lunch, still in the woods, I felt it. My pace was too fast. I waved my dad down and stopped. I tried to push through, but I threw up water, not food. A warning shot. I chalked it up to the medicine again, got back up, convinced I could "tough it out."

Shortly after, we reached a section of the trail that had been washed out. The soil was loose, and there was a raging river below. My quads were on fire, not from the incline, but from fear. Every step required full-body tension. My confidence cracked.

And then we saw it, the Hillary Suspension Bridge. The "Mother of All Bridges." It's the highest and longest suspension bridge on the trek, hanging 410 feet above the river. Built in honor of Sir Edmund Hillary, it represents progress, persistence, and the human spirit. But crossing it felt like walking into a storm.

The wind tore through the gorge as we stepped onto the narrow metal planks. Prayer flags fluttered wildly, snapping like whips in the air. The drop-off was steep enough to turn your stomach. I couldn't stop thinking of every movie where a bridge failed at the worst moment.

And then, I lost it, again. I threw up my lunch just before we crossed. I was horrified. Desperately trying not to look anyone in the eye. I knew what they were thinking: *altitude sickness*. But I knew it was dehydration and that it was catching up with me.

My quads gave out entirely after crossing. I collapsed in a heap, trembling. My triceps and even my fingers began to cramp. A kind group of Germans offered me electrolytes, grateful strangers trying to help. I accepted. But it was too late. My body was locking down.

I tried to stand, made it ten steps, then collapsed again. Ten more. Then again. Every muscle felt like it was turning to stone. My dad and Prashant huddled quietly, discussing what to do. I could see them glance my way, then back at each other. That's when the word "horse" first entered the conversation.

I'd reached my limit. I had to let go of ego and accept help. That's one of the hardest parts of leadership no one talks about—being strong enough to receive support when you need it most.

Prashant made the call. A local horseman appeared from the trees like a mirage, leading a small, lean mountain horse that looked more like a pony than a steed. It was clearly saddled for someone about 70 pounds lighter and six inches shorter. My knees jutted out like awkward wings. I felt like Ichabod Crane on his haunted ride through Sleepy Hollow, towering and wobbly and utterly out of place. But I didn't care. I didn't even have the strength to care. I was just grateful that relief was coming. That someone, or something, was going to help carry the burden I could no longer shoulder.

The horse moved with the sure-footed confidence of a local, weaving along the rocky trail as I swayed in the saddle like a scarecrow. I could feel the animal's discomfort beneath me, but my own discomfort had become white noise. Pain and shame blurred into numbness, replaced by the single, growing truth: *I would make it to Namche.*

When we finally reached Namche Bazaar, I didn't collapse on a bench like I'd imagined I might. Instead, I was met by the owner of our tea house, who must have seen the state I was in from a distance. Without hesitation, she walked straight to me, took me gently by the arm like a family member, and guided me to a seat inside. No questions. No judgment. Just kindness.

She returned moments later with a steaming cup of lemon tea, placed it in my hands, and gave me a nod that said, *You're safe now.* I can still feel that moment, the warmth of the cup, and the way it grounded me.

About thirty minutes later, my dad and Prashant appeared around the corner, winded but smiling. My father's face, a mix of relief and pride, was a sight I didn't realize I'd been waiting for. And Prashant, steady as ever, gave me that half-smirk that said, *You did it, didi.*

I hadn't walked into Namche.
I hadn't conquered the trail.
But I had made it.
And I was still in the fight.

We'd splurged on an upgraded room with an electric blanket and private bathroom, worth every rupee. It turned out the electricity shut off around midnight, but the blanket's warmth lingered long enough to make sleep possible.

Namche was a bustling amphitheater carved into the mountainside, with narrow alleys, bakeries, and teahouses all stacked like Lego blocks on the slope. It felt alive, like a base camp for ambition.

That night, we shared a plate of French fries covered in salt and reviewed the day. The worst was behind us, or so we hoped.

Leadership isn't always about pushing through. Sometimes, it's about stepping back, receiving help, and trusting others to carry you when you can't carry yourself.

MINDSET CHECK
Are You Leading or Just Enduring?

There's a fine line between pushing through and breaking down. In this chapter, I learned the hard way that endurance without adaptation is just ego in motion. The trail from Phakding to Namche didn't reward toughness, it demanded awareness. And it punished every moment I ignored the signals.

So here's your moment to step off the trail and check your own elevation; your mindset, your pace, your pride.

Ask yourself:

- Where in your life or leadership are you white-knuckling it? Are you pushing past your limits because you're afraid of looking weak?
- Are you listening to your body, your team, or your gut,or are you overriding it with ambition?
- What would it look like to recalibrate? Not quit. Just adapt. Change the pace. Ask for help. Take a breath.
- Who have you been unwilling to receive help from? And what would it take to shift that?
- Is your current strategy sustainable, or just survivable?

Sometimes leadership means going farther. But sometimes it means stopping before you collapse. It means receiving kindness—whether from a stranger with electrolytes, a guide with a plan, or a horse that shows up when your legs give out.

Your resilience isn't in how long you endure. It's in how well you adjust.

Check your mindset. Shift your frame. Reclaim your pace. *Because the goal isn't just to reach the summit. The goal is to still be you when you get there.*

Day 2 Elevation Profile: Phakding to Namche Bazaar

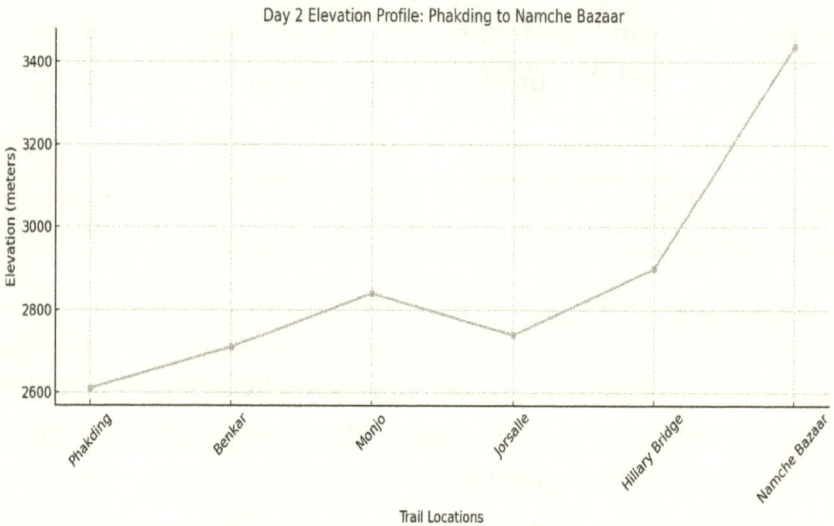

Karma and Acceptance

There's a stillness in the Khumbu that's hard to explain until you've walked through it. It's not just the quiet of snow-muffled paths or the absence of cars or motorcycles. It's a deeper stillness, a kind of internal silence that settles over you the higher you climb. It hums underneath every monastery bell, every whispered prayer wheel, every slow-burning juniper fire. And in that moment of quiet, I began to see something subtle but powerful: a kind of calm endurance in how people accept what is.

In the West, when something goes wrong, our instinct is to fix it. Push harder. Find the workaround. There's always a strategy, a shortcut, a fight to win. We resist discomfort. We deny uncertainty. We act like control is our birthright.

But here? The trail teaches a different lesson.

Flights into Lukla get canceled. Altitude sickness doesn't care about your training. The weather shifts without warning. A landslide can reroute your plans. And when it does, no one gets angry. No one yells at the sky. The locals just shrug and say, "Sometimes happy, sometimes sad. Sometimes sunny, sometimes cloudy." And beneath that shrug is something deeper: karma.

Not the simplified Western version, some cosmic reward system where good deeds earn good outcomes. Karma here is about balance. Cause and effect. The understanding that we're not in control of everything, and we were never meant to be.

I asked Prashant once if he ever got frustrated with the constant unpredictability, delays, dangers, detours. He smiled gently and said, *"We don't ask why the mountain changes. We just change with it."*

That stuck with me because so much of my life, especially post-military, has been about trying to reassert control. Trying to rebuild, to plan, to prepare for every possible outcome. But up here, control is a myth. And when you finally accept that, when you stop fighting the the terrain, your own limits, that's when the real clarity comes.

Karma, in this place, doesn't feel like punishment or reward. It feels like alignment. Like learning to live in step with something older and wiser than you. Like surrendering, not out of weakness, but out of respect.

And acceptance? That's the doorway to peace.

I didn't come to Nepal looking for a spiritual lesson. I came for the challenge, the beauty, the story. But somewhere along the trail, in the shadow of stone stupas and beneath skies torn wide open by prayer flags, I realized that maybe this was the story all along.

Not one of conquest.
One of acceptance.

MINDSET CHECK
Are You Fighting for Control or Flowing with Reality?

There's a kind of peace that only arrives when you stop trying to control everything. In the Khumbu, that peace doesn't come through victory, it comes through *alignment*. Through surrender. Through acceptance that the mountain, and life, will shift without your permission.

So let's pause. Not to fix or force, but to *assess*.

Ask yourself:

- Where in your life are you clinging to control that no longer serves you?
- What expectations are you carrying that are causing more stress than clarity?
- Are you mistaking resistance for resilience? Are you pushing when the real strength would be in pausing?
- When was the last time you simply accepted what is, without judgment, without spin, without shame?
- What might open up if you shifted from *why is this happening* to *what is this teaching me?*

Acceptance doesn't mean giving up. It means letting go of the illusion that you were ever steering the weather.

There's wisdom in loosening your grip. There's growth in surrendering to something older, deeper, and truer than your timeline.

Check your mindset. Release the need to control. Embrace the rhythm of reality.

Because sometimes, peace doesn't come from pushing through; it comes from *letting go*.

DAY 3
Acclimatization in Namche Bazaar – Adjusting to Altitude and Reflecting on the Journey Ahead

Mindset Shift: Sometimes, real strength lies in choosing the wiser path, not the hardest one. Leadership means knowing when to push and when to pivot.

After two long days on the trail, Day 3 in Namche Bazaar was our first real pause, a day to breathe, both literally and figuratively. At 3,440 meters (11,286 feet), Namche is more than a checkpoint on the trail to Everest. It's a suspended world, carved into the steep mountainside, where modern trekking culture meets ancient Himalayan life.

Namche appears almost like a hidden amphitheater built into the slopes, a terraced village that curves with the land. Its buildings are a kaleidoscope of deep blues, forest greens, and bright whites, their tin roofs catching the light like scattered mirrors. Below them, stone walkways zigzag between lodges, teahouses, bakeries, and gear shops, all stacked like layers on a mountain ledge. Prayer flags flutter above like multicolored veins in the sky, connecting rooftops and hearts with every breeze.

Despite the altitude, Namche buzzes with life. Yak bells echo off the stone walls. Children chase each other between the steps. And trekkers, weary but wide-eyed, shuffle through it all with a sense of awe.

One of the first things we learned was that hot water, true, glorious hot water, is a luxury not to be taken for granted. In

Namche, it's often cut off after 6 p.m., when the solar-heated tanks lose their warmth and the frigid air begins its nightly descent. A late shower is less "refreshing" and more polar plunge. We learned quickly: wash early, or brace for impact.

That morning, my father and I met with Preshant over warm cups of tea. We talked through the coming days, what lay ahead in altitude and effort. The next legs of the journey would be no joke: long stretches, thin air, and some of the steepest climbs yet. We were holding our own, but we knew the line between "hard-earned" and "high-risk" could thin just as quickly as the air.

So we made a call. We'd spend an extra day here to better acclimate. And when we reached Base Camp, we'd fly back down via helicopter instead of retracing our steps over the final 40 miles to Lukla. It wasn't a retreat, it was a recalibration. An act of wisdom, not weakness.

In the Army, we're taught to adapt, improvise, and overcome. But leadership isn't just about pushing through, it's about knowing *why* you're pushing and *whether* it's worth it. Sometimes the strongest move you can make is the one that lets you continue the mission safely, fully present.

With the new plan set, we could finally take in Namche at a slower pace. Our first stop was a steep 300-foot climb above the village to the Tenzing Norgay Sherpa statue, a quiet yet powerful monument that overlooks the town and offers one of the first true panoramic views of the Himalayan giants.

Tenzing stands mid-stride, ice axe raised in triumph, Everest just behind him, along with the rest of the Khumbu. Around him, the peaks stretch endlessly, Ama Dablam's perfect spire rising to the right, Lhotse and Nuptse stacked behind Everest like bodyguards, and Thamserku draped in shifting light and shadow. The wind picks up at the ridge, and the prayer flags snap behind him like a choir of silent witnesses.

Tenzing Norgay was born in the village of Thame, not far from here, in the Solukhumbu region. He was a man of the mountains long before he was a mountaineer, raised in the shadow of the very peaks he would later conquer. In 1953, alongside Sir Edmund Hillary, he became one of the first two confirmed people to summit Mount Everest, a feat that changed not just climbing history, but national identity. In Nepal, Tenzing is more than a hero. He is a son of the soil. A legend whose legacy lives in every porter's footsteps and every climber's dream.

His statue felt alive with that legacy. Strong, proud, and enduring, just like the people he represents.

Just a short walk away, we stepped into the Sherpa Culture Museum, a two-story stone building perched on the slope like a guardian of memory. The museum itself is modest on the outside, but inside, it's a treasure chest of artifacts, photographs, and stories that preserve the heartbeat of Sherpa identity.

One room recreates a traditional Sherpa home, complete with hand-carved furnishings, woolen blankets, and an open hearth. Another details the evolution of mountaineering in Nepal, showcasing vintage oxygen tanks, ice axes, crampons, and summit suits used on early Everest expeditions. Worn photos of Tenzing, Hillary, Messner, and other pioneers line the walls, alongside portraits of countless unnamed Sherpas who carried the burden of glory, literally and figuratively, on their backs.

The museum doesn't glorify the summit, it honors the journey. It shows how the Sherpa people have guided, supported, and in many cases, saved the lives of those attempting to touch the top of the world. It reveals their spiritual connection to the mountains, their reverence for the land, and their quiet pride in a role often overshadowed by the climbers they support.

That afternoon, I stopped at a local shop and bought a Sherpa-brand fleece. It was warm, lightweight, and just right for the changing Himalayan weather, a small but meaningful souvenir of this village carved into the sky.

And then, the cake.

The Namche bakeries are the stuff of trail legend. We'd seen them on every 20-something YouTuber's vlog, "Don't miss the carrot chocolate cake in Namche!", so of course, we had to try it. Part curiosity, part pilgrimage.

Let me tell you: it *lived* up to the hype. Rich, dense, impossibly moist, with a light chocolate glaze and just enough spice to warm your throat. After days of dal bhat and Snickers bars, this wasn't just a treat, it was a revelation. A little slice of civilization that felt hilariously out of place, and yet absolutely perfect.

Later, as the sun softened over the village, I saw from our dining area in the tea house, a dirt court near the edge of town where a group of young porters were playing volleyball, laughing, diving, yelling across the net like kids at recess.

Beside them stood a line of yaks, their heavy loads now removed, calmly chewing and watching the game unfold. Their wool was thick and matted, their eyes curious and unbothered. It was a surreal blend of labor and lightness.

That night at dinner, I replayed a few videos I had taken of the game earlier. I zoomed in casually and froze. There, in the background, leaping to spike the ball, was Robin, *my porter*. The same man who had carried my pack across suspension bridges and up steep stone steps, who had checked on me when I slowed down, whose job was to *carry* me through the hardest days, was out there playing like the trek hadn't even touched him.

A trip that had nearly broken me physically, and there he was, ending the day with joy and energy to spare. It was humbling and humanizing.

I realized, strength isn't always measured by how far you go or how fast you get there. Sometimes, it's about how fully you experience the place you're in. And how bravely you choose the path that aligns with your purpose, not just your pride.

That night, as the cold returned and the sky darkened to its signature Himalayan indigo, I felt something shift. Today wasn't just about adjusting to altitude. It was about aligning with the rhythm of the land, the people, and the reason we were here in the first place.

Today wasn't just about catching our breath at altitude. It was about taking stock. Slowing down. Seeing things more clearly.

MINDSET CHECK
Are You Climbing for Pride or Purpose?

In Namche, altitude forces a pause. But so does wisdom.

This chapter wasn't about summit fever. It was about clarity, realizing that sometimes the strongest decision isn't the one that takes you farther, it's the one that allows you to *keep going longer* and more meaningfully.

Leadership, like trekking, is less about speed and more about sustainability.

Ask yourself:

- Are you confusing intensity with impact? Are you pushing hard because you *should*, or because it truly serves your mission?
- Where in your life do you need to acclimate, not accelerate?
- Are you taking time to *observe* what's around you, or are you rushing toward a destination you haven't stopped to define?
- What version of success are you carrying, and is it still yours, or someone else's idea of achievement?
- Is it time to pivot your plan, not because you're weak, but because you're *wise*?

Namche reminded me: strength isn't always vertical. Sometimes, it's internal. Measured not in miles, but in moments of insight, alignment, and truth.

Check your mindset. Choose alignment over exhaustion. Let purpose, not pride, guide your pace. Because the goal isn't just to summit mountains. It's to stay grounded in *why* you started climbing in the first place.

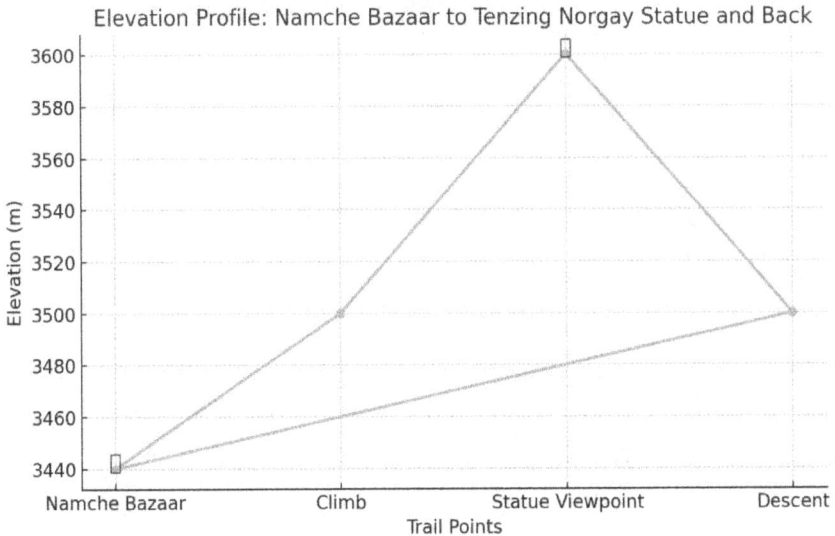

Elevation Profile: Namche Bazaar to Tenzing Norgay Statue and Back

Bistari, Bistari

"Bistari, bistari," Prashant would say, his voice calm and steady, whether we were grinding up a steep incline or just starting out after breakfast. Slowly, slowly. Then he'd add, almost like a mantra, "We walk at our own pace."

At first, I took it as encouragement. Maybe even a gentle warning. But over the miles, I began to realize it was something more, a philosophy of presence, not performance. A mindset born in the bones of these mountains.

In the West, slowness is suspect. We equate pace with value. If you're not pushing, grinding, producing, are you even trying? Something isn't working, and you will find yourself being asked, "Are you taking enough action?" That's the programming we inherit: Speed is safety. Hustle is heroism. Even in the Army, "speed is security" was drilled into us, again and again. And back home in civilian life, the tempo didn't slow, it just shifted into a different kind of urgency: more meetings, more noise, more striving.

But here, in the Khumbu, the air punishes those in a hurry. Push too fast, and the mountain will humble you. Climb too high too quickly, and you don't get a medal, you get altitude sickness. Out here, your body becomes your coach, your monitor, your limit-setter. The mountain doesn't negotiate with your ambition. It demands alignment.

At first, I fought it. I caught myself checking my watch. Measuring miles. Thinking about "making good time." But time doesn't work the same way here. The rules are different:

slower, older, wiser. You don't control the pace, you *tune in* to it.

When I finally surrendered to *bistari*, something changed.

I started to *see* more. Hear more. Feel more. I watched porters carrying loads twice their size, not in a hurry, but never stopping. I saw yaks plodding with calm authority, patient as saints. And I felt something shift in me.

This wasn't just about trekking. This was about identity. About the mindset of moving through life at a pace that honors your values, *not just your goals*.

It hit me how much of my life had been lived in a hurry. A rush to prove. A sprint to achieve. A hustle to outrun fear, doubt, failure. But *bistari* revealed a deeper truth: Some of our most important growth happens not when we're racing ahead, but when we slow down long enough to actually hear ourselves think.

This wasn't just about trekking smarter. It was about *living wiser*. Slowing down wasn't weakness. It was *mastery*.

I realized that in so many areas of my life—business, health, even healing—I'd been trying to accelerate transformation, instead of *allowing* it. But you don't build resilience in fast-forward. You don't cultivate clarity at sprint speed.

You have to *be* where your boots are. You have to let your soul catch up to your body.
You have to move bistari. And when you do, the mountain stops being a challenge to conquer, and starts becoming a mirror, a teacher, a sanctuary. So now, when I catch myself

racing the clock back home, when I feel that pull to "go faster" just to feel worthy, I think of Prashant.

I hear his voice: "Bistari, bistari. We walk at our own pace."

And I remember: the pace isn't the problem. The *urgency* is.

MINDSET CHECK
Are You Addicted to Speed or Committed to Presence?

There's a kind of strength that doesn't get celebrated in headlines or highlight reels: the strength to *slow down*.

In the Khumbu, I didn't just learn to pace my steps, I learned to pace my soul. And the hardest part wasn't the trail. It was unlearning the lie that urgency equals importance.

Ask yourself:

- Are you sprinting through life because you're scared of falling behind, or because you've actually defined where you're going?
- Have you mistaken momentum for meaning?
- Where have you sacrificed depth for speed, and what has it cost you?
- What would it look like to walk at *your* pace, not someone else's timeline or social media highlight reel?
- When was the last time you moved slowly enough to actually hear your own thoughts?

Bistari doesn't just change your pace, it changes your perspective. Slowness isn't laziness. It's alignment. Stillness isn't weakness. It's wisdom.

Check your mindset. Dial down the noise. Walk at your own pace. Because if you're always racing ahead ...you'll miss the view, the lesson, and the life right in front of you.

DAY 4
Onward to Everest View Hotel – A Rising Confidence and a Moment of Connection

Mindset Shift: The journey stopped being about reaching the destination and became about honoring the people beside me. Leadership wasn't about leading from the front, it was about walking together.

By the time we left Namche Bazaar to begin our second acclimatization day hike toward the Everest View Hotel, something in me shifted. The fog of self-doubt from those early altitude days began to lift. I wasn't just surviving the trek, I was stepping into it. With each stride, my confidence deepened. The Himalayas were no longer a looming challenge—they had become a place to be respected, not conquered. And we were moving deeper into them.

But it wasn't just the mountains that shaped the day, it was the people. My dad. Robin and Prashant. Me. Somewhere on that trail, we stopped being clients and guides. We became teammates. There was no hierarchy, just shared purpose. Each of us had our own reasons for being there, but now we were truly walking the same path.

The trail to Everest View Hotel starts with a jolt, no gentle warm-up. It rises out of Namche in sharp, switchbacking turns, on uneven rocky steps, climbing through a pine forest that offers little in the way of mercy. In the first hour, your lungs burn, your calves scream, and the trail tests your willingness to keep showing up.

It was in that stretch that my dad took his favorite photo of me.

No dramatic peaks behind me. No sweeping vista. Just me, slumped on the mountainside, sweat streaked across my brow, eyes glazed with exhaustion, body halfway folded under the weight of altitude and effort. It wasn't flattering. It wasn't triumphant.

But it was true.

That photo captured the moment the trek stopped being an adventure and started becoming something deeper. A test. A stripping away. It wasn't the mountain posing in the background, it was the mountain inside me, the one I had to keep climbing with every tired step. My dad loved that photo not because I looked strong, but because I didn't. Because it showed me showing up anyway.

As we climbed higher, the forest thinned. The air cooled. And then came the payoff.

Ama Dablam, sharp and proud like a shark's fin, stood to our right, graceful and intimidating all at once. Thamserku towered nearby, its massive shoulders blanketed in snow. Kongde Ri loomed across the valley. Then, finally, Everest herself appeared in the distance, her unmistakable summit just visible behind the sweeping ridge of Lhotse.

We stopped for breath, and not just because of the altitude. The view deserved reverence. The kind that stills your steps and stirs your soul.

We paused near Syangboche Airstrip, a narrow strip of earth perched impossibly high above the valley. It's not a commercial airport by any stretch, just a gravel landing zone built by Sir Edmund Hillary in the 1960s to support his school and hospital efforts in the Khumbu. It's rarely used now, but it still stands as a testament to his deep commitment to the Sherpa people after his historic 1953 summit.

Nearby, we passed a sculpture made entirely of recycled plastic trash, collected from the surrounding trails and repurposed into a hand. It was built by the Sagarmatha Pollution Control Committee, a reminder of what happens when privilege and tourism go unchecked. It was creative. Striking. And impossible to ignore.

Eventually, we reached the Everest View Hotel, a sleek, curved structure tucked into the mountainside, often hidden in cloud. Built in 1971 by Japanese entrepreneur Takashi Miyahara, it was never meant to be just a stopover for trekkers. It was designed for those who wanted to see Everest without having to trek to it. And some still do. Helicopters land daily from Kathmandu, delivering tourists who sip cappuccinos and eat lunch while staring at the peak from the terrace.

When I heard that, I turned to Prashant and laughed: "Man... that's cheating."

He grinned. "Maybe. But they still pay."

And pay they do. A scenic flight from Kathmandu to the Everest View Hotel, with a brief landing, can run $1,200 to $1,500 per person. That's the price of altitude without effort. View without the blisters. But sitting there with my boots unlaced, sweat-dampened sleeves rolled up, and a mug of tea in my hands, I knew the real reward wasn't the view. It was the journey that got us there.

We sat down together; Dad, Robin, Prashant, and me and shared a pot of tea. We bought for our guides not out of obligation, but out of respect. That moment wasn't about generosity. It was about unity.

In that moment, tea was a signal: we're not here to be carried, we're walking beside you. That's the kind of leadership that matters most when things get hard. Not rank. Not volume. Trust.

A framed Edelweiss flower on the hotel wall caught my eye. Small and unassuming, it has long symbolized alpine resilience. During WWII, it was awarded to German mountain troops, not for show, but for surviving the harshest conditions. It wasn't just a flower. It was a testament to endurance, sacrifice, and honor.

I shared that story with the group, and it landed with unexpected gravity. Edelweiss was a quiet badge of courage. Much like this trek, it wasn't about glory, it was about perseverance.

That moment reminded me of every soldier I'd known who led not with commands, but with quiet strength. The ones who carried weight without complaint. The ones who didn't need to be seen to matter.

And then, a small surprise: Pokémon Oreos in the hotel shop. Just a snack, but it hit hard. I thought of my kids. Bedtime stories. Saturday cartoons. Their laughter. I missed them. But that reminder reignited my "why." I wasn't just here for me, I was here to show them what resilience looks like. To show them their mom still knew how to climb. That she can still do hard things.

That night, my dad and I laughed until our sides hurt over the smell of our feet and a failed attempt at hygiene using lavender-scented "Dude Wipes." Several days in the same boots, it wasn't pretty. We called it a "10-wipe job."

Gross. Hilarious. Perfect.

Because trekking to Base Camp isn't just about summits, it's about what happens in between. The laughs. The tea. The symbolic flowers. The small comforts that keep you going.

This wasn't the hardest day. Or the longest. But it was a turning point. My confidence caught up to my ambition. My bond with Dad deepened. And my purpose became clearer than ever. I belonged on this trail. And I wasn't walking it alone.

Impermanence and the Sacred

The mountains don't speak in words, but they say everything.

By the time we reached the higher trails, past Namche, past the tree line into the barren beauty of the upper Khumbu, something began to settle in me. Not comfort. Not peace. Just truth. Unavoidable and clear.

Nothing here stays.
Not the clouds.
Not the snow.
Not the breath in your chest or the soreness in your legs.
Not even the trail itself.

You can round a corner and find it gone, washed away by a landslide or rerouted by weather. Porters build new cairns. Guides find new steps. And the trek continues. No one clings to what was. They just adjust and move on.

In the West, we build for permanence. Concrete. Reinforcements. Contracts. Calendars booked six months out. But here, even the mani stones, etched with prayers and stacked with care, are slowly being worn down by wind and time. The sacred here is not defined by how long it lasts. It's defined by the reverence with which it's lived.

I thought about that every time we passed a stupa, every time we ducked our heads to pass under a string of faded prayer flags, fluttering like echoes of devotion in the wind. The flags don't last. The prayers do.

That's the way of the Khumbu.

Everything changes.

And that is its beauty.

The weather turns in minutes. The views vanish behind a curtain of fog. A lodge that looked open might be shuttered by the time you arrive. You can't plan your way around that. You can only bow to it. Walk through it. Accept it.

I watched how the Sherpas moved with this truth built into their bones. They didn't push against the mountain. They walked with it. They knew the power of letting go, not as defeat, but as wisdom.

Impermanence here isn't failure. It's the fabric of the place.

And maybe ... of life.

In the military, I was trained to hold the line. To resist change. To lead through control. But the Himalayas have no interest in control. They break you open, not to defeat you, but to remind you: nothing is permanent, not strength, not struggle, not even suffering.

And that truth is not something to fear. It's something to honor.

Because if nothing lasts, then everything matters.

Every step. Every shared laugh. Every blister and every bowl of soup. Every look exchanged with my dad when neither of us needed to say anything out loud.

These moments don't have to be grand and evergreen. They took shape in the fleeting way the light hit Ama Dablam for just a few seconds before the clouds rolled in. The way a guide offers you a piece of chocolate without a word. The way your breath fogs in the cold before dawn, then disappears.

It made me wonder, what if the sacred was never meant to last forever? What if it's sacred because it doesn't?

Out here, I didn't cling. I noticed. I bowed. I kept walking.

And in doing that, I learned something I never could have grasped at sea level:

Some things aren't holy because they endure. They're holy because they don't.

MINDSET CHECK
Are You Leading to Be Seen, or to Walk Beside?

Somewhere between Namche and Everest View Hotel, leadership changed shape.

It wasn't about being out front. It wasn't about pushing harder. It was about *showing up*, tired, human, present, and choosing to walk *together*.

Leadership became a shared breath. A shared laugh. A shared cup of tea.

Ask yourself:

- Are you confusing visibility with value? Do you believe you have to lead from the front to matter?
- Where in your life are you trying to summit alone when the real strength is found in walking beside others?
- Are you carrying the weight of your mission with humility, or with ego?
- What would happen if you led with *presence* instead of pressure? With trust instead of control?
- When's the last time you shared the moment, not just the goal, with your people?

This chapter wasn't about reaching the hotel. It was about rising confidence. Humble leadership. Soul-alignment. The kind of leadership that honors the journey *and* the team.

Check your mindset. Redefine leadership. Share the weight. Honor the walk.

Because real leadership doesn't need a spotlight. It only needs your presence, and your people.

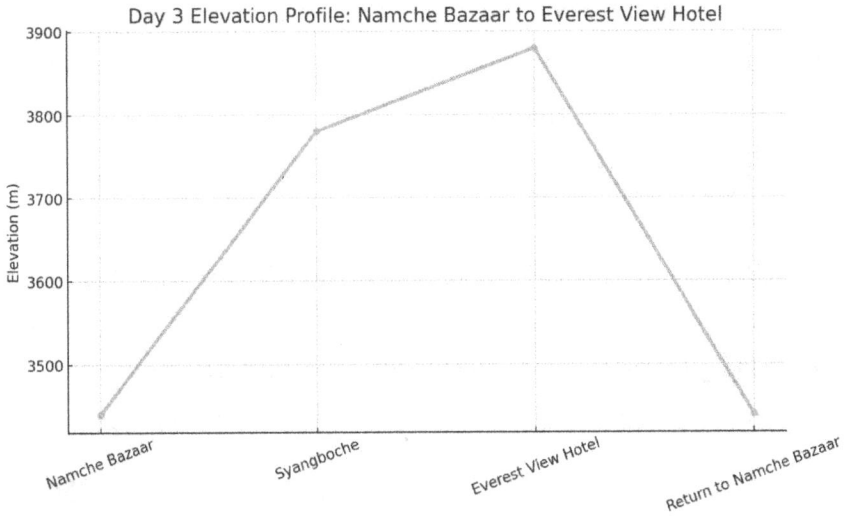

Day 3 Elevation Profile: Namche Bazaar to Everest View Hotel

DAY 5
Namche Bazaar to Tengboche – Views, Culture, and a Growing Sense of Accomplishment

Mindset Shift: From Commanding to Connecting – True leadership isn't about authority. It's about awareness, endurance, and the ability to move others forward, especially when the road gets steep.

Today marked a pivotal point in our journey as we trekked from Namche Bazaar to Tengboche. It was one of the most memorable days, where stunning scenery, cultural depth, and internal growth intersected on the trail. It felt like the mountain was no longer testing us, but beginning to teach us.

We began with a sharp, 20-minute climb out of Namche, one of those gut-check ascents that makes you question everything before the day has even warmed up. The town fell away behind us in layers: blue tin rooftops, winding stone paths, the scattered hum of morning life, and yaks meandering their way home. Once we cleared the ridge, the air opened wide, and so did the view.

Almost immediately, we stopped at a small white stupa adorned with prayer flags, honoring Tenzing Norgay Sherpa. He wasn't just the first alongside Hillary to stand on Everest, he was the heartbeat of what this region stands for. A local. A leader. A legacy. Standing there, I felt something deeper than admiration. I felt gratitude. Because Norgay's story isn't just about summits, it's about service. His greatness came not from conquering the mountain, but from carrying others toward it.

We pressed on, our boots crunching across sun-warmed gravel as the trail wove along the ridgeline. The views were absurd. Snow-capped titans emerged like sentinels through breaks in the clouds: Everest, distant but commanding; Lhotse, sharp and dignified; Ama Dablam, almost too beautiful to believe.

Ama Dablam, "Mother's Necklace," rises like a vision carved from cloud and ice—its steep, daggered face and outstretched ridgelines forming a natural embrace, both protective and severe. The name comes from the hanging glacier that drapes over its southwest face, said to resemble a *dablam*, the traditional pendant worn by Sherpa women to signify wisdom and protection. But there is nothing ornamental about this mountain. Her presence commands attention. She is not simply admired—she is honored, respected, and, at times, feared.

Standing at 6,812 meters (22,349 feet), Ama Dablam doesn't need to compete with Everest's height; her form alone makes her unforgettable. Towering above the trail from Namche to Pangboche, she arrests your gaze and refuses to let go. There's something almost sentient in her presence—as if she sees you before you see her. Climbers often speak of her as if she chooses who may approach and who must turn back. In the high Himalayas, where every peak is revered, Ama Dablam feels deeply personal.

The first successful ascent in 1961 by Barry Bishop, Mike Gill, Wally Romanes, and Sherpa leader Mingma Tsering marked a new era of technical alpinism in Nepal. Unlike Everest, which is often approached as an endurance feat, Ama Dablam is a mountaineer's mountain—narrow ridgelines, vertical ice, and exposed traverses that demand absolute focus and precision. The "Dablam" hanging glacier itself has claimed lives as it periodically calves off tons of ice onto the standard southwest route. To summit her is to walk a razor's edge between elegance and lethal consequence.

For the Sherpa people, she is more than a climb—she is sacred geography. Her image adorns prayer flags, walls, and temple murals across the Khumbu. Many believe she watches over the valley, especially over women and children, her necklace symbolizing not just beauty, but spiritual protection. Before any climbing expedition begins, a *puja* ceremony is held at base camp—prayers are offered, and blessings are sought from the mountain herself. No one climbs Ama Dablam without her permission.

When I stood beneath her shadow, I understood why. She wasn't just a mountain. She was metaphor—graceful and dangerous, maternal and untouchable. Her beauty was disarming; her sharp ridgelines cut through both landscape and illusion. You can't look at Ama Dablam and pretend you're in control. You can only stand there and understand that you've entered a place where the earth rises into the divine, and where your presence is temporary, conditional, and small.

Ama Dablam became, for me, the emotional center of the trek. Not the highest point, but the one that demanded the most reverence. Every view of her felt like a gift, every angle a lesson in strength and surrender. She is the kind of mountain that follows you home—not because you climbed her, but because you didn't need to.

Ama Dablam reminded me that nature doesn't just humble you. It refines you. It reminds you that beauty and hardship often share the same trail.

We descended through pine and rhododendron forests, the air perfumed with cedar and earth. We passed handmade bridges lashed together with rope and local wood, flexing under our weight but holding firm. Goats picked their way across the cliffs like seasoned climbers. Wildflowers peeked through the frost-thawed soil. Life here clings with quiet determination.

By now, I'd learned to fuel differently. Heavy foods didn't work. Soup did. Brothy, salty, hydrating, it was trail gold. My dad and I joked about how I was basically surviving on garlic soup and Snickers. And my Buff? Ruined. Stained beyond salvation from constant nose-wiping and trail grime. The Khumbu cough was real, and so was the amount of snot oozing from my nose. I wasn't winning any beauty contests on the trek, for sure. I was disgusting, and being able to laugh about it created some of the most hilarious memories with my father along the trek.

Meals were also getting more expensive the higher we climbed. A bowl of soup or dal bhat now cost around $8, but the meals tasted better than most $30 entrees back home.

After lunch, the trail turned cruel again. We crossed the Dudh Koshi River one last time and stared up at the switchbacks that led toward Tengboche, a brutal, unrelenting climb that made time feel slower and the air feel thinner.

It was somewhere in the middle of that grind that we passed three German women. They looked like they were moving in slow motion, heads down, arms limp, each step deliberate and strained. We gave each other that silent look trekkers exchange when it's hard for everyone. No small talk. Just mutual respect. We were all suffering our way up the same mountain. But in that moment, I was able to recognize and adopt a more deliberate pace. And in doing so, I went from needing to stop and catch my breath every 50 meters in elevation gain, to stopping every 20 minutes to rehydrate.

The mountains are full of surprises. Just ahead of us, one of the younger porters came around a bend, blasting Nepali pop music from a small speaker strapped to the side of his enormous load. He was jamming, literally bobbing his head to the beat, moving like he was on a victory lap instead of a 2,000-foot ascent. It was ridiculous. And awesome. And very humbling. The soundtrack was all joy, no struggle. I smiled despite the ache in my legs. That guy was carrying 80 pounds of gear and still had rhythm.

I realized that in environments like this, leadership reveals itself in rhythm. In small, consistent acts. In setting a pace others can follow, not forcing one they can't.

We reached Tengboche just as the weather turned. At this point, based on elevation, we were IN the clouds but it felt like they had descended like a curtain, cold and thick, obscuring the view and wrapping the village in silence. We were chilled to the bone, our sweat cooling fast as we pulled on puffer jackets and zipped everything tight. Tengboche Monastery stood a short walk away, its golden rooftop barely visible through the mist.

It cost just $3 to enter the monastery that day. But honestly? The warmth of the nearby tea house called louder than our curiosity. Our bodies ached. Our breath was shallow. We didn't talk it through; we just knew. A warm room, a mug of tea, and a shared laugh felt like the intentional choice at that moment.

Still, it's worth knowing: the Tengboche Monastery is the spiritual heart of the Khumbu. It's one of the most important Tibetan Buddhist monasteries in Nepal, home to about 60 monks who live, train, and chant here at the foot of the world's tallest mountains. For many Sherpas, this is where blessings are given before attempting Everest. It's a center of teaching, meditation, and ceremony, and one of the highest functioning monasteries on earth.

But for us, the special moment would not be found inside a monastery; it was our shared fatigue that needed no words.

We collapsed into our chairs and didn't move for a long minute. And when we finally did, it was only to pour more tea and laugh about the Buff again.

That night, I reflected on what the day had taught me. I was beginning to understand and learning to listen, to my body, to the trail, to the stories told by fellow trekkers and those etched into stone and snow. I was becoming a better teammate. A more patient leader. A more present daughter.

Real leadership isn't loud. It's consistent. It's kind. It moves others forward, even on the hardest days.

MINDSET CHECK
Are You Leading to Be Heard
—Or to Move Others Forward?

Tengboche reinforced an important lesson: *real leadership doesn't walk ahead for applause.* It walks beside, for endurance, for presence, for people.

This wasn't a day of commanding. It was a day of connecting, through rhythm, through struggle, through silent nods exchanged on switchbacks and joy carried by a porter with a speaker full of pop music and 80 pounds on his back.

Ask yourself:

- Are you setting a pace that others can follow, or one that only proves your strength?
- Are you listening deeply; to your people, your body, your environment, or are you pushing blindly through noise?
- Where can you lead with kindness instead of control? With consistency instead of force?
- Are you showing up for your team when it's hard, or just when it's convenient?
- What does leadership look like when no one is watching, and you're exhausted too?

This was the day I realized that every leader is also a follower, of pace, of trust, of a greater mission than themselves. And sometimes, the strongest thing you can do isn't lead from the front. It's to *stay in rhythm* beside someone who needs it.

Check your mindset. Match your pace to your people. Build trust with your presence. Lead through rhythm, not rank or position. Because real leadership doesn't demand that the trail bend to your will. It walks in service, *even when the air is thin and the climb is steep.*

Elevation Profile: Namche Bazaar to Tengboche

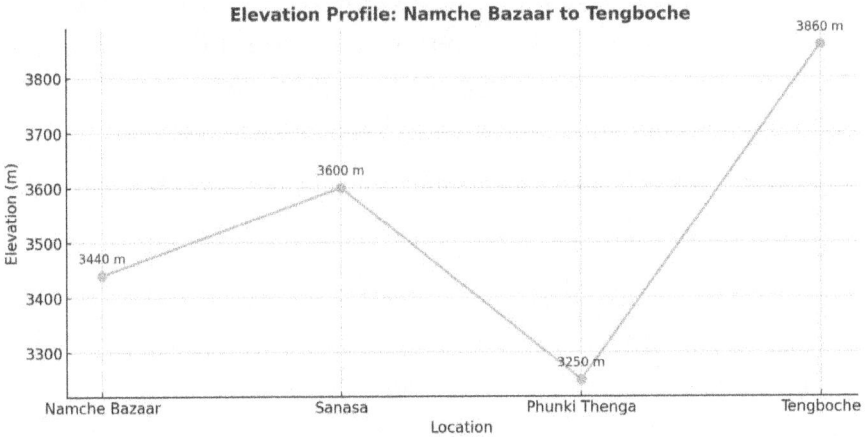

Stillness Without Structure

Mindset Shift: From Seeking Significance to Living It

We didn't go into the monastery.

We were right there, at the foot of Tengboche Monastery, one of the most significant spiritual sites in all of Nepal. For centuries, monks have trained, prayed, and offered blessings to climbers on this ridge. Their chants echo through the mountain's thin air. Their devotion is stitched into the trail. This place is more than a building, it's a threshold between the physical and the spiritual. And yet... we didn't go in.

Not out of irreverence. Not because we didn't care. But because our bodies had reached their edge. Our feet ached. The wind had turned sharp. The clouds were closing in. We were cold, depleted, and craving the simple comfort of warmth and stillness. The monastery could wait. The feeling we couldn't quite name—but knew was real—would be there tomorrow. Our bodies needed attention *now*.

At first, I felt a flicker of guilt, like I'd skipped a required rite of passage. But as we sat in the tea house nearby, boots unlaced, steaming mugs cradled in tired hands, I realized something I hadn't expected: I hadn't missed the sacred. I had just found it somewhere else.

It was in the quiet between our words. In the slow exhale of survival after a brutal climb. In the way my dad smiled when I unwrapped another Snickers bar and called it dinner. It was in the clinking of metal cups and the shared sense of *we made it*. In that moment, I wasn't outside holiness, I was sitting right in the middle of it.

In the West, we're trained to associate the sacred with formality, architecture, ritual, and rules. You wear the right clothes. You enter with quiet reverence. You sit when you're told, stand when expected, kneel on cue. The sacred becomes something we access through structure and permission.

But here in the Khumbu, the sacred is everywhere. It lives in effort, in stillness. In the way light shifts through the clouds over Ama Dablam. In the steady rhythm of boots on stone paths. In the silent respect Sherpas show when passing a chorten or spinning a prayer wheel with a bowed head. There are no instructions here. No one announces that you're standing on holy ground. You just feel it.

I came to understand that it wasn't about a destination or a temple—it was about how I showed up. It was awareness. The kind you earn through exhaustion. The kind you learn by walking, not reading. The monastery mattered. Of course it did. But so did that tea house. So did the silence between sips. So did the aching legs and the shared fatigue that didn't require a single word.

We never made it inside that day. But I believe something divine made its way into me. A quiet shift. A deepening. A realization that the sacred doesn't require robes or walls. It requires attention. It requires presence. That moment beside my father, cold and laughing and grateful, was a cathedral of its own. The sermon was stillness. The offering was tea. The altar was a table between two people who had earned the right to sit down.

And that was enough.

MINDSET CHECK
Are You Looking for the Sacred, or Already Standing In It?

There's a difference between chasing meaning and *noticing* it. In Tengboche, I learned that the sacred doesn't always wait behind carved doors or under golden roofs. Sometimes it arrives disguised as a cup of tea, a shared silence, a long exhale after the climb.

Ask yourself:

- Where in your life are you waiting for permission to feel awe or reverence?
- Have you mistaken the sacred for the structured, and missed what's already right in front of you?
- When was the last time you sat in stillness long enough to feel the holiness of the moment, not the environment?
- Are you treating rest, connection, and presence as less important than performance, achievement, or ritual?
- What if sacredness wasn't a place to get to, but a way to pay attention?

That day on the trail, I learned that reverence simply needs your awareness. It needs your willingness to see beauty where you are, not where you think it's supposed to be.

Check your mindset. Loosen your grip on where the sacred is "supposed" to live. Open yourself to the holy in the humble.

Because sometimes, what you thought was a detour...was actually the sanctuary.

DAY 6
Tengboche to Dingboche – Leading Through the Clouds

Mindset Shift: *From Strength to Stillness – Leadership is not just about charging forward. Sometimes, it's about walking slowly, staying grounded, and leading by example when visibility is low.*

The trail from Tengboche to Dingboche marked a literal and figurative shift. We had entered high-altitude territory, and with it came a slower, more deliberate pace. The air was colder, thinner, and wrapped in mist. The world around us blurred. Clouds rolled over ridgelines, obscuring peaks we had come to rely on for direction. In their place: stillness.

The terrain felt heavier underfoot. Every breath took effort. We crossed suspension bridges strung over rushing rivers and followed narrow switchbacks through fog-cloaked stretches of mountain. Everything felt surreal. Like we were walking through a dream, or a memory.

Somewhere along the way, we passed a locals-only trail that cut almost straight up the mountainside, so steep it looked nearly vertical. I instinctively braced for a challenge, tightening my pack straps. But Prashant turned and grinned: "Not this one. This is a locals-only trail." I laughed out loud, the tension releasing like a knot undone. We stayed on the gentler route.

That moment reminded me how important it is to trust those who know the terrain better than you.

Prashant was showing me, leadership sometimes means knowing which paths not to take and trusting someone else to guide you through the unknown.

As the hours passed, the landscape changed. We were now above the treeline. The tall pines and rhododendron forests of lower elevations had vanished, replaced by low scrub bushes, rock, and wind. Gone were the trees. More stone. Fewer people. More solitude.

And the altitude? It was taking a toll.

We were now over 14,000 feet. Our blood oxygen saturation, which would hover near 97–99% at sea level, had dropped, somewhere in the mid-80s for most of us. Every breath felt like half a breath. We moved slowly, not from lack of will, but from biology. The human body wasn't built for this height, but it adapts, one step, one breath at a time.

That day, I noticed something else: the yaks.

We'd seen them before, but now, they were everywhere, hauling supplies, walking beside porters, lounging near stone huts. Their massive lungs and thick coats make them perfectly adapted to this altitude. But they're more than just pack animals.

To the Nepali people, especially the Sherpa community, yaks are revered. They're providers of milk, butter, meat, and wool. Their dung fuels the stoves in tea houses, a vital source of heat where trees no longer grow. They carry gear up to Everest Base Camp and beyond, forming the backbone of life and logistics in these high places. But they also hold spiritual significance.

Yaks are often decorated during festivals. Their presence in prayers and traditions is a reminder of the Sherpa philosophy: live in harmony with the land, respect what sustains you, and waste nothing. Watching them work, calm, powerful, essential, I found myself silently grateful for them. Without yaks, this trail wouldn't function. And neither would we.

Now that we were above the treeline, that reverence became even more obvious. There was no firewood. No trees meant no traditional fuel. Everything warm, every pot of tea, every brief flicker of heat, was powered by dried yak dung. It was collected, shaped, dried, and stacked like firewood around stone huts. It didn't smell great, but it didn't smell bad either. One thing I quickly realized was that it didn't burn long. But it was everything. Without it, there was no warmth. No meals. No life. It was a reminder that survival here depends not on comfort, but on connection to the land and its rhythm.

We eventually stopped for a break at 4410 Café, a gem in the middle of the mountains. Warm drinks. Fresh desserts. A short looping video on Sherpa culture played in the corner. I sipped ginger tea while wrapped in my down jacket, the warmth a welcome contrast to the cold outside. These tea houses, like small outposts from another world, reminded me of combat outposts during deployments—rough around the edges, but vital. They weren't perfect, but they were enough. And just like those outposts, they offered small luxuries that felt disproportionally comforting: familiar food, a place to rest, and in many cases, the chance to charge your electronics. Some tea houses allowed free charging at the table, others offered limited battery boosts or a plug-in fee—but even that felt like a miracle at altitude. The ability to top off a phone or headlamp battery connected us, not just to the trail, but to something steady amid all that elevation and exposure.

It was starting to sink in with me that resilience isn't always loud. Sometimes it's a stove fueled by dung, a yak load tied with a fraying rope, or a café that plays a documentary when your oxygen is low and your spirit needs lifting.

When we reached Dingboche, perched at 14,305 feet, it felt like the edge of something vast and untamed. The air was razor-thin, crisp in a way that scraped the inside of your lungs. Our tea house offered shelter, but no real warmth. The common room held a single stove at its center, fed with pressed rounds of yak dung. Each evening, the staff would light a single burn—just enough to take the edge off the cold while dinner was served. Then, the fire was left to die down, conserving fuel for the days ahead. It was practical, but unforgiving.

Of all the tea houses we stayed in, this was the coldest. The walls seemed to breathe cold. Even layered in down, there was no lingering near the stove after hours. We spent more time in our room here than anywhere else on the trail, tucked into our sleeping bags with the electric mattress pad cranked as high as it would go. It buzzed faintly beneath us, a small miracle of modern comfort against the Himalayan chill. In a place where even boiling water froze overnight, that blanket felt like armor— a barrier between exhaustion and the elements.

Dingboche wasn't the most hospitable stop, but it was one of the most memorable. It asked us to recalibrate what "comfort" meant, and we answered with quiet routines: layering up, zipping down, tucking in early. It was survival softened by small kindnesses—ginger tea, veggie egg and rice, and that blessed hum of warmth beneath the sheets.

Food and conversation came slow. So did movement. But so did presence. There was something comforting about knowing that nothing here was wasted, not fuel, not breath, not kindness.

And speaking of kindness, Prashant had quietly taken it upon himself to carry all our extra snacks in his pack. Apples. Pomegranate. Cookies. He'd pull them out when the moment called for it, like a magician with a backpack full of morale. I devoured the fruit like I'd been on a three-day fast. My dad, ever consistent, went straight for the Snickers, mainlining that familiar hit of chocolate and sugar like it was trail medicine. It wasn't planned, but it was perfect. It reminded us both that small comforts carry big weight up here.

And speaking of real-world adjustments, this was also the part of the trek where the toilets became a gamble. If the water pipes weren't frozen, you might get a flush. But more often than not, you had to fill the toilet manually using a nearby bucket of cold water. If that wasn't humbling, I don't know what was. High-altitude plumbing is just another lesson in gratitude.

That night, as the cold settled in and the lights dimmed, I found peace in the slowness. In the absence of sound. In the simplicity of breath and blankets, and being beside someone who had taught me how to lead long before I ever wore a uniform.

You don't have to see the summit to know you're leading. Sometimes, you just have to keep walking, one quiet, deliberate step at a time.

MINDSET CHECK
Are You Leading Loudly, Or Living Your Leadership Quietly?

The higher we climbed, the quieter everything became. The path narrowed. Peaks faded into clouds. And yet, leadership didn't vanish, it simply shifted form. It stopped being about direction and started being about presence.

This was leadership by stillness. By rhythm. By resilience. Not the kind that draws attention, but the kind that *carries others through*.

Ask yourself:

- Are you measuring your leadership by how visible you are, or by how grounded you feel?
- Do you only feel valuable when you're moving fast, or can you find meaning in slowing down?
- Who in your life is watching how you endure, not just how you perform?
- Where are you being asked to steady the group instead of steer it?
- What kind of leader do you become when the map disappears and the fog rolls in?

That day, I learned that you don't have to see the summit to keep others moving forward. Sometimes leadership looks like choosing the gentler trail. Sometimes it's handing out fruit when morale dips. And sometimes ... it's just putting one foot in front of the other without making it about you.

Check your mindset. Walk with steadiness. Lead through presence. Choose the quiet strength that holds others steady. Because leadership isn't always about seeing what's ahead, sometimes it's about staying strong when no one else can.

The Hallowed Struggle

Up here, struggle isn't a detour, it's the trail.

By the time we reached Dingboche, we had left behind the conveniences of lower elevations. No more flushing toilets. No more firewood. No more fast, full breaths. Everything had to be earned: heat, food, rest, progress. Even laughter took effort.

But that struggle, surprisingly, didn't feel like failure. It felt... sanctified.

The cold no longer felt like an inconvenience. It felt like a teacher. The thin air didn't feel cruel, it felt like a test I was supposed to face. The simplicity of life at this height, just breath, warmth, food, and people, stripped everything else away until only the essentials remained.

And in that stripping away, I found something I didn't expect: meaning.

I've spent most of my life trying to reduce friction. Planning. Controlling. Avoiding unnecessary hardship. But up here, hardship isn't optional. The altitude doesn't care about your schedule. The mountain doesn't care about your goals. And the tea house certainly doesn't care if the water bucket you're using to flush the toilet is cold, or if the pipes are already frozen. Spoiler alert, in March, they often are.

Everything is harder. But everything matters more.

Soup tastes better when your body needs it to function. The quiet feels richer when there's nothing left to say. The sight of someone sharing a chocolate bar or pouring hot tea for others isn't small, it's a respected act.

That's what this place has taught me: discomfort isn't something to run from, it's something to walk with.

It clarifies. It prioritizes. It humbles.

And strangely, it connects. There's a quiet intimacy in shared struggle. My dad and I didn't need to process every hard moment out loud. We just looked at each other, nodded, and kept moving. Our bond wasn't built in conversation, it was built in mutual perseverance.

The same was true with our guides. With strangers on the trail. With the porters jamming out to Nepali pop while carrying loads twice their body weight. No one here is trying to impress anyone. We're all just trying to keep going. And that makes every act of kindness, every shared snack, every offered seat, every hand on a shoulder, feel like worship.

Struggle, when shared and respected, becomes a binding act. A crucible. It becomes a ceremony of endurance, of quiet leadership, of trust.

We often look for meaning in mountaintop moments, summits, sunrises, and epiphanies. But maybe the real transformation happens in the middle, when you're tired, cold, and unsure... and you choose to take one more step anyway.

That choice, the step, the breath, the presence, is profound.

Not because it's perfect.
But because it's honest.
Because it costs something.
And because it brings you closer, not just to the summit, but to the people beside you and the version of yourself that you've been trying to meet.

MINDSET CHECK
Are You Running from the Struggle, or Walking with It?

At altitude, struggle isn't an interruption, it's the invitation.

In Dingboche, we stopped asking *"Why is this so hard?"* and started asking *"What is this teaching me?"* The cold, the simplicity, they didn't punish us. They revealed us. And in that revelation, we discovered that the most meaningful parts of the journey were forged in the hardest places.

Ask yourself:

- Are you avoiding discomfort, or honoring it as part of your growth?
- Where have you mistaken struggle for failure, when it's actually transformation?
- Are you numbing the pain of challenge, or letting it sharpen your priorities?
- When was the last time you gave meaning to difficulty, instead of trying to escape it?
- Are you showing up in the hard moments with presence, or just waiting for them to pass?

This wasn't just about enduring for endurance's sake. It was about *making peace with our trek*. Because when the goal stops being comfort and starts being *connection*, everything shifts. Every act of kindness becomes intentional. Every shared burden becomes a bond. And every hard-earned step becomes a prayer.

Check your mindset. Respect the struggle. Step with intention. Share the weight.

Because what breaks you open...might be the very thing that sets you free.

DAY 7
Acclimatization Day in Dingboche – Presence Over Progress

Mindset Shift: From Momentum to Presence – Sometimes progress isn't forward. It's inward.

Above 4,000 meters, something shifts. The air is so thin. The pace slows. Distractions fall away. What's left is what's real; your breath, your footsteps, and the people beside you.

Dingboche was our stop for acclimatization, a day meant to hike higher, then return to sleep low. It's a proven strategy to help the body adjust to altitude. Most trekkers climb 500 meters on this day. It's the standard approach. But my dad and I chose a different route. We climbed only 300 meters. Not because we couldn't do more, but because we didn't need to. For the first time, I allowed myself to believe that *being here was enough*. We weren't here to suffer for sport or perform for photos. We were here to experience something real.

Somewhere along the trail, we passed the famous rock outcrop, the one where trekkers dangle off the ledge, arms outstretched, trying to capture that perfect "on the edge" shot with a Himalayan backdrop. It's iconic. And earlier in the trek, I might have wanted that photo too. But in that moment, I didn't have it in me. My focus had shifted. I didn't need to hang off a rock to prove anything. I just wanted to sit beside my dad and watch the clouds roll through the valley.

We found a patch of stillness among mani stones and prayer flags, tucked beneath the towering grace of Ama Dablam. The clouds drifted like breath across her face. It was profound, not because it was extreme, but because it was quiet, honest, and ours. At one point, I pulled out my camera and captured Prashant dancing in the clouds, Ama Dablam behind him like a frozen wave. His joy was effortless. The moment, breathtaking. But even those stunning images couldn't quite capture what we were feeling. Because what mattered most was that we were *there*, and fully present, fully alive, in one of the most beautiful places on Earth. No filters. No performance. Just joy.

The trail to Nagarjun Hill that morning had begun in cold wind and a shifting sky. The route wasn't technical, but at over 4,000 meters, altitude made every step becomes a negotiation. Legs moved, but each one asked for permission. And somehow, that challenge felt right. Not forced. Not competitive.

Above the treeline, everything must be carried. Blankets. Propane. Rice. In the lower villages, donkeys do the work. Up here, it's yaks. Patient, purposeful, powerful creatures that move without urgency or complaint. Watching them, I saw something familiar. Yaks don't chase speed or attention. They carry, steadily, without praise or reward. I've known Soldiers like that. Men and women who shouldered impossible weight, silently. Strength that doesn't make headlines, but moves mountains.

And I realized I had more in common with the yaks than I'd like to admit. I've spent most of my life carrying invisible weight, the kind no one sees, the kind you don't put down because someone has to bear it. Like the yaks, I kept moving. Not for recognition. But because the load mattered.

That day, we learned that our porter, Robin, wouldn't see his family again until monsoon season. His quiet dedication reminded me of young troops I'd served with, steady, selfless, and far too familiar with separation. Prashant told us his father had been a guide before him, and his mother still worries when he goes into the Khumbu. But his father? He understands. Because it's the job. That, too, felt familiar; the quiet strength of families who wait, who support, who serve behind the scenes.

As we climbed, those stories echoed through me. Sherpas. Soldiers. Porters. Yaks. All connected by service. All willing to carry what others can't. At the ridgeline, the clouds finally parted. Ama Dablam. Lhotse. Island Peak. Nuptse. They didn't erupt into view; they *emerged*, like a slow reward for patience.

That moment taught me something I hadn't expected: leadership doesn't always mean pushing forward. Sometimes, it means holding still. Listening. Pacing the team so no one gets left behind. On the way back down, I kept watching the yaks. Their breath visible in the cold, their pace unbothered. They didn't need applause. They just moved forward.

So did we. Not fast. But forward.

MINDSET CHECK
Are You Measuring Progress, or Just Movement?

At altitude, everything slows: your breath, your pace, even your ambition. And in that space, something deeper opens up; the truth that not all progress moves forward. Some of it moves *inward*.

This wasn't the day for glory shots, or aggressive climbs. It was the day we learned that presence isn't a pause in the journey; it *is* the journey. And the strongest leaders aren't always the ones out front. Sometimes, they're the ones who sit still long enough to hear what actually matters.

Ask yourself:

- Where in your life are you chasing motion instead of meaning?
- Are you climbing for validation, or sitting in the sacredness of the moment?
- Who are you becoming when you slow down long enough to *feel* it?
- Are you carrying weight that no one sees, but refusing to put it down because it matters?
- Is your leadership about pace, or presence?

That day on the ridgeline, surrounded by clouds and prayer flags, I saw leadership in Prashant. In the silent strength of our porter, Robin. No titles. No noise. Just steady movement, deep service, and the kind of resilience that doesn't need to be seen to be real.

Check your mindset. Slow down. Get quiet. Walk with intention.Because forward isn't always faster, and stillness might just be your strongest move.

The Gift of Discomfort

I've never been someone who glamorizes pain. I know the trifecta of misery well: no sleep, no food, and bone-deep cold. I've been on missions that made national headlines, grinding through the hours when all I wanted was to sleep. And just when you think it can't get worse, it does. Because the only thing that makes that trifecta truly complete... is being wet. Soaked, shivering, and still responsible for people and decisions that don't care how depleted you are.

I've been there. I've felt the ache in my joints, the static in my brain, the slow suffocation of discomfort that presses down and refuses to lift. I've gritted through the physical stuff and sat inside the kind of mental discomfort most people would do anything to avoid. And yes, I've grown. But the growth never came *during* the pain. It came *after*. After I got still. After I came down. After I had the time and clarity to reflect, ask better questions, and finally let the lesson rise to the surface.

That's why I've always carried a quiet tension with people like David Goggins. Not because I don't respect him, I do. Deeply. He's endured more than most of us could ever fathom, and his message has real power. But Goggins has a rare gift. Pain is his fuel. He runs toward the darkness and builds a home there. That's not a criticism. That's reverence. But it's not how I'm wired, so it will never work for me.

For me, discomfort isn't the destination. It's the doorway. And on this trek, especially in places like Dingboche, where the air was razor-thin and the cold crawled through every layer, I came to realize something: discomfort can teach you, *but only if you stop treating it like the enemy.*

It reveals your edges. Shows you where your coping begins, where your ego gets loud, where your compassion shuts down. It doesn't break you. It introduces you to the version of yourself that doesn't need applause or certainty to keep moving. Not to shame you, but to refine you.

There were moments on the trail when that introduction felt sharp and clear, my stomach light, chest tight, every step across frozen rocks a small negotiation. A dull headache pressed against my skull. My breath was uneven and ragged. And yet, we continued to move. Because we were moving for clarity. No, I didn't become a machine. I became more *human.*

That's what this trek reminded me: I don't need to chase suffering to grow. I don't need to build a brand around pain. But when discomfort shows up, and it always does, I can sit with it. I can learn from it. And when the cold lifts and the light breaks through, I can carry what it gave me into what's next.

That's the gift. Not the pain itself. But the perspective it leaves behind.

MINDSET CHECK
Are You Avoiding the Pain, or Learning from It?

There's pain that crushes. And there's pain that clarifies. Discomfort is never the point, but it can be the portal.

Most of us are conditioned to avoid it. We plan, prep, and protect ourselves from hardship at all costs. But when discomfort shows up anyway, uninvited and unavoidable, we have a choice: shrink back, numb out... or lean in with a sense of curiosity.

On the trail and in life, pain doesn't ask for permission. But it often carries a lesson if you're willing to pay attention.

Ask yourself:

- When discomfort hits, do you brace and power through, or pause and *listen*?
- Are you using pain to prove something, or to *learn* something?
- What do you believe discomfort says about you? Weakness? Or invitation?
- Where are you mistaking suffering for failure, when it may actually be formation?
- What have you carried quietly for too long... and is it time to understand why?

On this trek, I didn't chase pain. But I stopped resisting it, too. I let it slow me down, strip things away, and introduce me to a more honest version of myself. Not tougher. Not colder. Just more real.

Check your mindset. Stop avoiding the discomfort. Start honoring the message. Because pain is rarely the destination, but it might be the trailhead to the person you're becoming.

DAY 8
Trek to Lobuche: Memorials and the Weight We Carry

Mindset Shift: *From Visibility to Legacy – Leadership isn't always seen. It's felt in the choices you make when no one's watching, in the lives you honor, and in the stories you carry forward.*

The trail from Dingboche to Lobuche wasn't the most technical, but it carried a different kind of strain. A silent gravity that settled in your chest as you walked, not from the altitude alone, but from the memory and meaning embedded in the route.

The morning hike was steady and unhurried. We passed stone huts and windswept pastures, signs of seasonal yak herders who survive at the edge of the world. There was a kind of purity in the landscape, stark, stripped-down, and humbling. It mirrored something inside me. Fewer distractions. More clarity.

Eventually, the trail led us up a steeper climb to Thukla Pass, a place I knew was coming, but nothing could prepare me for it.

And I mean that quite literally, because for a few minutes, I lost the trail entirely.

Somehow, in my determination to keep a good pace, I found what looked like a worn footpath leading through a jumble of rocks. It made sense ... at first. Until it didn't. Before long, my dad and I were full-on bouldering. And not in the cool, Instagrammable way.

No, we were scrambling up unstable rocks at 15,000 feet, huffing like old locomotives, both of us wondering how the actual trail had apparently vanished into thin Himalayan air.

My dad, to his credit, said nothing. He just followed. Carefully. Probably questioning every life decision that had brought him to this moment, including trusting me with the route.

At one point, I looked back at him, hands on a granite ledge, one knee up, breathing like he was climbing Everest itself, and I thought, *"This might be a bit much."*

I glanced over and caught Prashant watching us from the real trail, twenty feet to our left and ten feet lower, with a look I can only describe as *gentle pity*. Then, with quiet grace, he took the lead. No scolding. No judgment. Just a subtle course correction.

And honestly? I was so grateful. Leadership isn't about always being right. Sometimes it's about realizing you've led your team into a field of boulders, admitting it, and getting the hell back to the real trail.

By the time we reached the top of the pass, no one had died. We were back on solid ground. And the humor had caught up with the altitude.

It wasn't my best moment as a navigator. But it became one of my favorite stories because it reminded me that leadership isn't about ego. It's about adaptability, forgiveness, and letting someone else take the reins when they know the terrain better.

We rejoined the trail, legs burning, breath shallow, and followed Prashant's lead without a word. His steady, unspoken guidance said more than any correction ever could.

Looking up from below, I had seen the silhouettes, from what I assumed were a handful of memorials clustered near the ridge. I didn't realize there would be what appeared to be hundreds, maybe even thousands. As we crested the hill, the trail opened into a wide plateau—endless stone beneath a breathless sky.

The memorials stretched in every direction. Some were towering stacks of carved granite. Others were simple piles of rocks with names barely legible, weathered, forgotten, but still standing. The sizes spanned generations, the stories unspoken, but felt.

Lined across the ridge were dozens of stone memorials, cairns built for those who never returned from the mountain. Climbers. Sherpas. Some names were famous. Most were not. But all had carried the same dream: to reach something greater than themselves. Some paid the ultimate price.

We stopped at Scott Fischer's memorial, his name familiar from *Into Thin Air*. It was surreal to stand there, knowing his story, but what struck me more were the memorials with no fanfare. Simple stones. Quiet markers for the backbone of every expedition.

This was the heaviest part of the trek. Not because of the climb, but because of the weight of memory. These people gave everything, not for glory, but for the mission. For the summit. For others. That's legacy.

I couldn't help but think of the soldiers I've known, those who didn't come home, and those who came home different. Their stories often go untold. But they echo through places like this.

The Sherpa community has begun to speak more openly about the cost they carry. About the imbalance between the recognition given to foreign climbers and the sacrifice borne by those who make their success possible. It's a hard truth. And a necessary one. Because legacy doesn't come from reaching the top. It comes from honoring those who made it possible to even begin the climb.

When we finally reached Lobuche, something in me lightened. I broke into a goofy little song, "We're at Lobuche! Champions!" Both Robin and Prashant laughed. Even my dad cracked a smile. It was a small moment of joy. And after the weight of Thukla Pass, it felt earned. Sometimes leadership is lightness, the courage to break tension with humor. To make space for joy, even when the load is heavy.

But Lobuche was no celebration. It was cold, stark, and high, at 4,910 meters (16,105 feet). And that night, the pipes froze completely.

Which meant that when nature called, you were on your own. No flush. No running water. Just you, a bucket, and whatever frozen plumbing you could navigate in the dark. This is the part YouTube influencers don't show you. The glamorous trekker vlogs don't film this. But it's real. And it was disgusting.

This was the edge of comfort, and it stripped away any illusion of control.

And yet, in the middle of that discomfort ... I looked around and realized something unexpected: *I was in the most beautiful place I'd ever been.*

I've lived in western Montana. I've spent time in Glacier National Park, some of the most breathtaking terrain in the United States. I've stood atop Pikes Peak, learned to ski in the Colorado Rockies, and hiked countless trails through alpine ridgelines and glacial valleys.

But nothing, and I mean nothing, compared to this.

No matter which way I turned in Lobuche, all I could see were incredible Himalayan peaks, sharp and endless, their ridges catching the wind like sails. Snow whipped off their summits at such speed that it looked like smoke, or clouds being born. I stood there and watched weather systems form before my eyes, shaped in real time by the raw force of the mountains.

It's hard for that not to change you.

And in that moment, I felt immense gratitude for the opportunity, for my body, for the chance to stand in this place. We had enjoyed incredible weather on this trek, clear skies, only two partially cloudy days, and views that most people never get to see. I know how rare that is. And the magnitude of that gift is not lost on me. Not now. Not ever.

During this stretch, Prashant shared something beautiful with me. I had asked about a phrase he repeated often: *"Sometimes happy, sometimes sad. Sometimes sunny, sometimes cloudy."*

He smiled and told me it came from a popular Nepali song called "Resham Firiri." He claimed he didn't have a beautiful voice, but in that moment, he sang anyway. Soft, off-key, and pure. It was a kind of joy that didn't need polish to be real.

That's the thing about this altitude, it strips you down. Not just physically. Emotionally. Spiritually. You can't fake it here. You're either real or you're quiet.

This is also right about the time when the altitude started to catch up with us.

Until now, we'd managed. The climbs were hard, but they ended. The breathing was labored, but recoverable. But in Lobuche, it wasn't just during the trek that we felt it. It was all the time, even when we were sitting still.

I noticed a French couple near the pot-bellied stove that contained the tea house's fire, just sitting, but breathing like they'd just run up a hill. Then I looked around and saw other trekkers doing the same. Then I looked at my dad. We were doing it too. Sitting by the stove, trying to get warm ... but struggling to breathe.

It didn't matter if you were in your 20s or your 60s. Science didn't care. This air had nothing left to give. And it was clear: this was not a place the human body was designed to thrive.

In all my reading about Everest, one concept stuck with me: the Death Zone, the altitude above 8,000 meters (26,247 feet) where the human body can no longer acclimate. Where death becomes a matter of time. You may summit, but you will not survive there for long.

We weren't in the Death Zone. At Lobuche, we were just over 10,000 feet below it. And I could feel that truth, this wasn't a place meant for the average person to stay. It didn't carry the name "Death Zone," but it didn't feel like it had given us an open invitation either.

That evening, I stood outside, bundled in every layer I had, and watched the sun begin to set over Nuptse. The cold clung to my face, but I stayed still, not wanting to miss the moment. The light shifted from gold to amber, then to that sharp, blue-edged gray that signals nightfall in the high Himalayas. Nuptse's massive ridgeline, dark and jagged, caught the last light like a blade catching flame. It doesn't get the same attention as Everest, but Nuptse is a monster of a mountain.

Rising to 7,861 meters (25,791 feet), its flanks are steep, broken, and avalanche-prone—a wall of ice and rock that looms over the Khumbu like a warning. Its name means "West Peak" in Tibetan, but the moniker feels far too modest. Nuptse doesn't seduce climbers with fame; it dares them. While Everest draws crowds with the promise of glory, Nuptse remains wild and unwilling, its summit rarely touched, and only by those with the skill and luck to survive her shifting slopes. It's not just difficult—it's untrusting.

You don't summit Nuptse. You negotiate with her, briefly, if she lets you. It's not a goal—it's a boundary. A reminder that some mountains are not meant to be conquered. As I stood there, watching her silhouette grow sharper against the fading sky, I felt less like a trekker and more like a witness. Nuptse was a sentinel, not a prize. A mountain that stood watch over this valley like a stone guardian—unmoved, unreadable, and unapologetically untamed.

She made Everest feel almost accessible by comparison. Not smaller, not less imposing—but somehow, more known. More mapped. Nuptse remained untouched in a different way—aloof, as if belonging to another realm entirely, one that didn't care for summit photos or personal bests. In her presence, I felt humbled, not in the cliché sense of awe, but in the raw sense of being measured—and found small.

That night, I lay in bed thinking not about reaching Base Camp, but about what it meant to walk among giants. Mountains like Nuptse weren't just landscapes. They were mirrors. They showed you how much noise you carried inside. How much ego you tried to bring with you. And then they stripped it away, without permission or apology.

And I let them. Because something in me knew that what I was carrying couldn't be taken to the summit anyway. Not by weight, but by spirit. Nuptse didn't want to be climbed—she wanted to be respected. And in that moment, respect looked like stillness, like presence, like knowing when to simply stand and look up.

And in that golden moment, as the sun hit its icy face and turned it to flame, I stood still. Breathing shallow. Heart full. This was not a place for performance. It was a place for reverence. And I was grateful just to be there. Just to witness it. Just to endure it, shoulder to shoulder with my father, and know that this, right here, was part of the legacy I would carry forever.

MINDSET CHECK
Are You Leading to Be Seen, or to Be Remembered?

There's a moment on the mountain when you stop trying to reach the top and start asking what you'll leave behind.

Lobuche wasn't about performance. It wasn't about pace. It was about legacy. Quiet. Earned. Shared. It showed up in the memorials at Thukla Pass, in the unspoken bond between guides and porters, in the recognition of lives lost, and lives quietly carrying on.

Ask yourself:

- Are you leading for recognition, or for the impact that outlasts you?
- What are you building that others will carry when you're gone?
- When no one's watching, how do you show up?
- Who are you honoring, not with words, but with the way you walk?
- Can you accept that leadership isn't always a summit, it's sometimes just staying steady in the cold, the altitude, and the quiet?

This wasn't a chapter of control. It was a chapter of surrender. Of following someone else's lead. Of course correction without shame. Of reverence for people whose names may never be known, but whose sacrifices built the trail.

It was also about lightness, humor in high places. Joy after weight. The kind of laughter that only comes after survival. That, too, is leadership.

Check your mindset. Let go of the need to be visible. Lean into the power of legacy. Because leadership isn't about being out front. It's about what still echoes when you're gone.

Elevation Profile: Dingboche to Lobuche

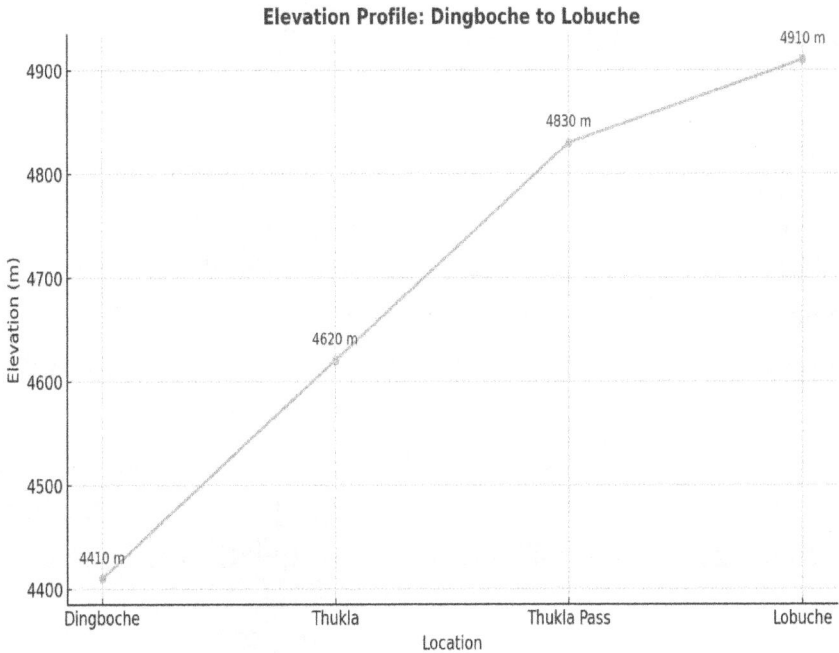

Not Built to Stay

Lobuche felt different the moment we arrived. Not just higher. Not just colder. It felt temporary. Like everything around us, the trail, the tea house, even ourselves were simply passing through. The warmth in the walls was short-lived. The fire in the stove didn't last. Conversations grew quieter. Movements slowed. Even laughter felt like it had to be rationed, as though we were all silently acknowledging the same truth: this is not a place you linger.

And that's because it isn't.

Perched at over 16,000 feet, Lobuche sits in a space between worlds, above the treeline, well below the Death Zone, but fully inside the realm where the body begins to rebel. This isn't where people live. It's where they pause. It's where breathing takes effort, even while sitting still. Where even the most athletic people look just as drained as the rest of us. It's the kind of place where science begins to argue with spirit, where acclimatization and willpower wage a quiet, invisible war in your chest.

There's no thriving here. Only passing through. And that hit me harder than I expected.

So much of my life has been built around endurance, digging in, pushing through, holding the line. In the military, in leadership, in life, I've trained myself to stay in hard places longer than most. But Lobuche reminded me of something I hadn't fully internalized until then: not every hard place is meant to be stayed in.

Some environments exist to teach you, not to house you. Some struggles are designed to refine you, not to define you. And some elevations are meant to be touched, but never lived in.

That truth didn't feel like failure. It felt like freedom. Permission. Permission to move on. To listen to your breath, your body, your gut when it whispers, *"This is enough."* To recognize that just because you've arrived doesn't mean you're meant to plant roots.

Standing in Lobuche, I saw the beauty in that impermanence. The raw wind. The sound of nothing and everything. The weathered, scarred faces of the mountains. This place was beloved precisely because it was fleeting. Because no one, not even the strongest, could stay for long.

In a world that constantly urges us to grind longer, push harder, and outlast everything, Lobuche offered a different kind of wisdom: know when to move on. Know when strength looks like stepping away instead of staying put. Know when leadership means saying, "This place shaped us. But we're not built to stay here."

MINDSET CHECK
Are You Staying Because You Should, Or Because You Don't Know How to Leave?

We're taught to hold on. Push through. Outlast.

But what if real strength isn't staying longer than everyone else?
What if it's knowing when the altitude has done its job, and it's time to move on?

Lobuche stripped away the illusion of control. It reminded us that some places are *meant* to be uncomfortable, not to punish us, but to teach us. And once the lesson is learned, the leadership is in the leaving.

Ask yourself:

- Where in your life are you staying out of habit, not purpose?
- Are you confusing endurance with alignment?
- What's the cost of clinging to a place that was never meant to hold you?
- Who are you becoming by trying to prove you can outlast something that no longer serves you?
- And what would it look like to say: "This shaped me, but I'm not built to stay here"?

The world will tell you to stay. To grind it out. To prove your toughness by hanging on.

But sometimes, the real act of leadership is letting go, with clarity, not shame.

Check your mindset. Let go with honor. Move forward with wisdom. Because not every high place is a home, some are just waypoints on the journey to who you're becoming.

DAY 9
Everest Base Camp: The Final Push

Mindset Shift: From Doubt to Determination – Leadership isn't the absence of fear; it's choosing to take the next step anyway.

The morning we left Lobuche, the air felt thinner, both physically and emotionally. The pipes in the tea house had stayed completely frozen overnight. No flushing, no running water, and a brutal truth: the higher you go, the less your body, and basic plumbing, cooperates. I'm still mad no one talked about it on the YouTube videos.

But there was a tension to the day that went deeper than discomfort. This was it: the final push. Every step would bring us closer to Everest Base Camp, the goal that had drawn us halfway around the world. But even in that excitement, doubt crept in.

The trail from Lobuche to Gorak Shep is short in distance, barely three kilometers, but at over 16,000 feet, "short" doesn't mean "easy." In fact, we were moving at one kilometer per hour. Just think about that: 1 km/h. You could outwalk us with a slow shuffle through a grocery store. But it was all we could manage. Every step felt like hiking through wet cement while someone gently pressed on your chest.

At altitude, speed disappears. What's left is intention. Precision. And the willingness to keep moving when every cell is begging you to stop.

As we trudged slowly forward, Prashant began pointing out the distant peaks, naming them one by one like old friends: Pumori, Lingtren, Changtse—and behind them, Tibet. That caught me off guard. It felt surreal, being able to see into another country, another world. I had been so focused on each step, each breath, that I hadn't realized how far we'd come—or how much the world had opened around us. The landscape was barren now, stripped of almost all vegetation, the ground crunching underfoot with gravel and ice.

Prayer flags whipped in the wind, strung between cairns and chiseled memorials that reminded us how unforgiving this place could be. Then Prashant lifted his trekking pole again and motioned toward a sharp wall of stone and shadow rising just beyond the glacial moraine. "Lhotse," he said quietly. I followed his line of sight—and there it was, emerging above the chaos of the trail like a blade pulled from the sky. Cold, sheer, and commanding. The wind picked up as we paused, and I found myself standing still—not just to catch my breath, but to take in the weight of that name. We were surrounded by giants, but this one felt different. Lhotse didn't ask to be admired. She simply existed—watching us, measuring us, saying nothing at all.

Lhotse doesn't court fame the way Everest does. She doesn't have to. For those who know the mountains, Lhotse is a purist's peak—raw, sharp, and unforgiving. The mountain earned its reputation not only for its height—8,516 meters (27,940 feet), the fourth-highest in the world—but for its nearly vertical South Face, one of the largest walls of exposed rock on the planet. Towering more than 3,000 meters from base to summit, it's a feature so daunting that it wasn't successfully climbed until 1990, decades after the main summit was first reached in 1956 by Swiss climbers Ernst Reiss and Fritz Luchsinger. The delay wasn't from lack of trying—it was from the mountain's sheer unwillingness to cooperate.

Most trekkers don't realize that Everest and Lhotse are quite literally connected at the hip. They share the same route up to Camp III before the paths diverge, Everest angling northwest toward the South Col, Lhotse veering southeast into a steep, unforgiving couloir. From a distance, they appear like neighbors. In reality, they're two peaks bound by the same backbone, a single massif split into two radically different personalities. Everest may be the tallest, but Lhotse is the one that whispers, *Only if you're ready.*

From the trail between Lobuche and Gorak Shep, Lhotse reveals none of her history, but all of her presence. The closer you move to Base Camp, the more the landscape opens, and the more Lhotse seems to rise in defiance of gravity itself. Her flanks are steep, broken, and ice-scoured, catching late afternoon light in a way that turns them molten for a moment, only to swallow it into shadow seconds later. Unlike Everest, which often hides behind her own shoulder or behind Nuptse's broad ridgeline, Lhotse stands exposed—blunt and unfiltered, like a truth too sharp to soften.

And yet even as Lhotse held my gaze, something in the air tugged me forward. Just beyond Gorak Shep, the trail narrowed and climbed slightly, winding along the edge of a frozen world that felt less like earth and more like a threshold.

Then it came into view—the Khumbu Icefall—sprawling, immense, and otherworldly. It didn't just rise from the glacier. It emerged—like something alive.

This wasn't just a glacier. It was a creature.

The Icefall sat at the foot of Everest like a massive, sleeping beast, built not of flesh and bone, but of ice towers, crevasses, and shifting fear. It didn't simply exist. It lurked. Watching. Choosing. It was the first real gatekeeper of Everest, and before climbers even touched a fixed rope or clipped into a ladder, they had to face this—a force that didn't care who they were or how badly they wanted the summit. This was the first moment every climber had to ask themselves, not "Can I do this?" but "Do I truly want this?"

Seracs the size of apartment buildings leaned into one another, fragile and waiting. The glacier groaned under its own weight, even in stillness. It didn't move like a mountain. It breathed—deep, ancient, and slow. Every few hours it reshaped itself, swallowing ladders, collapsing walls, opening crevasses like mouths. Climbers move through it before dawn when the cold tightens the ice, hoping to buy a few hours of mercy. But even then, the margin is razor-thin.

In 2014, sixteen Sherpas died here in a single instant—buried beneath a collapsing section of the Icefall while fixing the route for others. Their names are etched into the stones not far from the path, and still, the Icefall shifts above them, unchanged.

This is where the climb begins. Before Base Camp truly ends. Before the altitude breaks you. Before the summit dreams take shape. The Icefall decides who moves forward.

Standing there, I wasn't climbing it—but that didn't seem to matter. The Icefall saw me anyway. It sees everyone. It doesn't need your reverence. It demands your surrender. And it gives nothing back.

Prashant stood quietly beside me and pointed toward the heart of it. "This is the most dangerous part," he said, his voice low. "And it's only the beginning."

I didn't speak. I just stood there, staring at the frozen chaos. Not with awe, but with a kind of reluctant understanding. You don't conquer a place like this. You pass through it on borrowed time—if it allows.

This was something I had read about for years. Studied. Watched in documentaries. A place that belonged to legends, not to me. And now ... it was right in front of me.

The glacier stretched like a frozen river of jagged white and blue, cracked and creaking under its own weight. I felt a lump in my throat. This wasn't just terrain. This was history. This was the breath of the mountain made visible. Something about standing there made me feel incredibly small and impossibly lucky.

Emotion caught me off guard again as we moved toward Base Camp. The last three kilometers were brutal, less a trail, more a boulder field dumped by giants, scattered with patches of snow and winding, uneven footing. But in the distance, we could finally make out the camp itself.

Tents dotted the glacier, yellow and orange specks barely clinging to flat space on the ice. Upon reaching Everest Base

Camp, we were greeted by the iconic boulder marking the site, traditionally adorned with hand-painted red letters stating "EVEREST BASE CAMP – 5364m." However, in March 2025, the scene was different from the images I'd seen before. The rock had been heavily vandalized, with the original inscription obscured by layers of graffiti, scratches, and overwriting. This defacement was jarring, transforming a revered landmark into a canvas of disorder.

The motivations behind such vandalism are varied. Some individuals protest the use of the name "Everest," a colonial designation assigned by the British. The mountain's original Tibetan name, Chomolungma, translates to "Goddess Mother of the World," holding profound spiritual and cultural significance for local communities. For them, the imposed name "Everest" diminishes this heritage. However, defacing the landmark disrespects the sanctity of this place and the collective achievement it represents for trekkers worldwide.

Adding to the scene, a wooden signboard had been erected near the boulder to commemorate the 70th anniversary of Sir Edmund Hillary and Tenzing Norgay's historic ascent. While intended to honor this milestone, the signboard's placement and the ongoing vandalism sparked controversy among visitors and conservationists, highlighting the tensions between preservation, commemoration, and personal expression at this historic base for dreamers and climbers.

Despite these alterations, the profound significance of reaching Everest Base Camp remained undiminished. Standing before the weathered boulder, amidst the fluttering prayer flags and the towering peaks, I felt a deep connection to the countless adventurers who had stood there before me, each drawn by the mountain's timeless allure.

A few steps later, Prashant handed us each a scarf, green, not white, like the khatas I had seen earlier in the trek. It was a symbol of congratulations and blessing, a moment I'll never forget. I held it in my hands and felt overwhelmed. It wasn't just fabric. It was a moment. A recognition. A reminder that we had made it.

My dad celebrated the only way he knew how: he tore into a Snickers bar, grinning like a kid. "Victory Snickers was a welcome reward," he said between bites. "Not nearly as rewarding as the victory helicopter ride home tomorrow." I laughed harder than I expected. The best part? I caught the whole thing on video. It still makes me laugh every time I watch it.

And yet, for all the celebration, I knew this was a place that demanded deep respect.

People training to summit Everest don't just "show up" here. They spend weeks at Base Camp, slowly acclimating. Climbing up to Camp 1 and back. Then to Camp 2 and back. Then higher. Over and over again. Their bodies have to adjust to each new altitude, each wave of thin air and strain. They live here—on a moving glacier, surrounded by shifting ice, battered tents, and the constant low rumble of the mountain adjusting herself beneath them.

Climbers call it the *rotation cycle*: hike high, sleep low, stress the system, then recover. It's methodical. Brutal. Necessary. If they move too quickly, they risk high altitude pulmonary or cerebral edema—fluid in the lungs or brain. If they move too slowly, their bodies deteriorate under the weight of exposure and attrition. This place takes something from everyone, even before the climb truly begins.

And then there's the cost. Financially, summiting Everest can cost anywhere from $40,000 to over $100,000 per person. Permits alone are thousands. Add to that the guiding company, oxygen bottles, insurance, gear, logistics, Sherpa support, and weeks—sometimes months—away from home, career, and family. You don't just pay for Everest with your bank account. You pay for it with your life as you know it. And sometimes, with your actual life.

Walking through Base Camp, I passed climbers taking care of their feet, checking O2 tanks, refreshing weather forecasts like their lives depended on it—because they did. Some looked calm. Others looked wrecked. But none of them looked casual. They had all said yes to something enormous. And in May they would all be waiting for a two-day weather window to decide if that yes was going to be enough.

And the thing is—even Base Camp isn't safe.

People think once you've reached it, you've made it. Like it's the safe zone at the edge of the board. But Everest doesn't work that way. This mountain doesn't care where the tents are pitched or whether you came to summit or just to see. Base Camp is still the mountain's terrain. And it still takes.

In 2015, when a 7.8 magnitude earthquake struck Nepal, it triggered a massive avalanche off Pumori. The snow and ice slammed into Base Camp with staggering force. Entire camps were leveled. Tents ripped apart. Climbers and Sherpas were buried beneath debris. At least 22 people died that day—right here, at the supposed safe place. The images from that tragedy are hard to forget. Helicopters lifting out the injured. Survivors walking dazed through snowfields that hours earlier had been bustling with preparation and planning. Everest made no distinction between veteran climbers and first-time trekkers. It never does.

Even without earthquakes, Base Camp is a place of slow erosion. The glacier beneath your feet is melting. Shifting. Breathing. At night, you can hear it creak and groan. Sometimes tents collapse under snow. Sometimes altitude sickness hits someone unexpectedly, and evacuation becomes urgent. Every step here is earned, and every breath is negotiated. There's no such thing as casual.

So while Base Camp might be the goal for thousands of trekkers each year, it is not a guarantee. Not of safety. Not of survival. Not of anything, really, except the opportunity to witness this mountain up close—and decide what that means to you.

And for me, standing there, that decision was clear. I didn't need to go higher. I didn't need to press further to validate the journey. Seeing the Icefall up close, feeling the glacier shift beneath my boots, standing in the shadow of tragedies past— that was enough. More than enough.

Because Base Camp isn't the end. It's the beginning of a conversation with something much older, colder, and more honest than most of us are ready for.

And the most courageous thing I could do in that moment wasn't to push forward.

It was to stand still. And listen. The summit isn't the only place where transformation happens. Sometimes, it happens at the edge, where you get close enough to see what it takes, and decide to honor the mountain without needing to conquer it.

Somewhere on the return to Gorek Shep from Base Camp, I broke. The fatigue and the emotional weight of the trek, it all caught up to me. I had to stop and cry. Not a dramatic moment. Not a meltdown. Just tears behind sunglasses, as the wind howled and the trail kept stretching forward.

Leadership under pressure doesn't always look brave. Sometimes it looks like crying while climbing. Like letting the emotion pass, and then keep moving anyway.

That's what I did. I moved anyway. We didn't stay long. The altitude and cold wouldn't allow it. The way back to Gorak Shep was a blur. I remember the wind, the ache in my legs. And feeling equal parts accomplished along with a little sad the adventure with my dad was over. Then there was the squatty potty where I brushed my teeth because the pipes were still frozen. That helped a little with being sad. I also remember tying my boots and seeing my Apple Watch record it as an "active minute." It made me laugh. Barely. But I'll take it.

That night, in the thinnest air I'd ever breathed, wrapped in layers of blankets, I stared at the ceiling and let it all sink in.

Base Camp wasn't just a destination. It was a reminder.

Of how far we'd come.

Of what we'd carried.

Of who we'd become along the way.

Reaching Base Camp taught me this: Leadership is resilience under pressure. It's compassion when others falter. It's belief when the summit is still far off. And above all, it's the ability to hold your mission, even when your body and mind want to let go.

Base Camp was never the end. It was the moment I remembered who I am.

MINDSET CHECK
What Do You Do When the Mission Demands More Than You Think You Have?

There's a moment on the mountain, somewhere after the last reliable breath, before the finish line, when your body says no. Your lungs tighten. Your legs wobble. Your spirit flickers. And you hear that quiet voice inside say, *"You can stop here."*

And you don't.

That's the moment this chapter is about.

The last three kilometers to Base Camp weren't just hard—they stripped me down. Not the kind of hard you power through with a motivational quote. The kind that wears away at you slowly, quietly, when no one's watching. And maybe that's where the real transformation happens—in the moments that don't need an audience, where you're forced to meet yourself exactly as you are.

Leadership under pressure doesn't always roar. Sometimes it looks like tears behind sunglasses. Sometimes it's a shaky step forward. Sometimes, it's choosing *not* to quit when no one would blame you if you did.

Ask yourself:

- What's your Base Camp? What dream or goal are you crawling toward when everything in you wants to tap out?

- When have you mistaken slowing down for failure, when it was actually strength?
- What edge are you standing on right now, and who are you becoming because of it?
- Can you allow yourself to break *without* backing down?
- Do you believe resilience means never falling apart, or getting up again after you do?

This wasn't about conquering Everest. It was about honoring the mountain, *and the version of myself that kept walking toward it, even when it hurt.*

Check your mindset. Leadership isn't loud at altitude. It's quiet. Steady. Unshakable.
Not because you didn't doubt. But because you *moved anyway.*

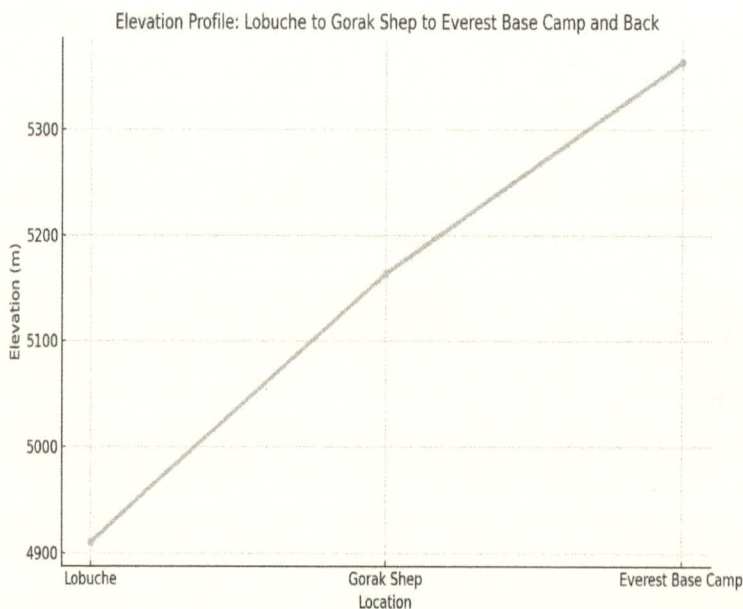

Elevation Profile: Lobuche to Gorak Shep to Everest Base Camp and Back

Sāthiharu: Walking Together as a Way of Being

In Nepali, the word for friends, sāthiharu, carries more than camaraderie. It comes from *sāthi*, meaning companion, and *haru*, a plural suffix. But in the mountains, it doesn't just mean "friends." It means *those who walk with you.*

It's a word rooted in tradition and meaning. A trail word. A reminder that in the Khumbu, to travel together is to be bound by something deeper than schedule or destination. Shared hardship creates a kind of spiritual gravity. It's our crucible that tests us, that we are able to pull from when the discipline won't cut it on its own, and you have to reach into yourself for pure willpower.

On the trail to Everest Base Camp, that truth becomes crystallized. We weren't just a group anymore. We had become sāthiharu, not because we said it, but because we lived it.

In the West, we often romanticize the lone climber. The solo entrepreneur. The self-made leader. But in Nepalese culture, interdependence is not a weakness, it's a wisdom. You don't walk ahead of your group to prove strength. You stay in rhythm, in relationship, in *sangha*, a spiritual fellowship.

"In the Himalayas, walking together is more important than arriving first. Because arriving alone is not arriving at all."
—*Sherpa proverb*

Even the physical design of the trail honors this mindset. Prayer flags aren't hung in isolation. They stretch across paths, from tree to tree, rooftop to rooftop, *always connecting*. Mani walls, those long, stone-carved slabs marked with prayers and ancient teachings, aren't placed on peaks. They're placed in the middle of the path, where everyone walks past them together. They're not meant to be climbed. They're meant to be acknowledged *as you pass through, together*.

And every chorten, every prayer wheel, every hand-carved stupa is turned with a clockwise spin, not for personal gain, but as an act of collective merit.

That's what I began to understand when we took our photos on top of the Everest Base Camp rock. We hadn't just climbed. We had *shared the climb*.

Leadership in that moment wasn't about position. It was about *presence*.

The Nepali way of moving through the world, quiet, reverent, community-centered, offers a lesson so many of us in the West forget: We were never meant to summit alone.

And the summit isn't just a place. It's a bond. A shared rhythm. A trail well-walked, with *sāthiharu* by your side.

MINDSET CHECK
Are You Walking Ahead, Or Walking With?

Western culture glorifies the lone wolf. The solo hiker. The leader who climbs faster than the rest and plants a flag at the top. But in the Khumbu, that's not how greatness works. The depth is found in walking together.

Sāthiharu doesn't just mean friends. It means those who *walk with you*, those who match your pace when you slow-down, who walk beside you when all goes quiet inside, and who remind you that the summit isn't the reward. *The relationship is.*

Ask yourself:

- Who are your sāthiharu, and have you told them what they mean to you?
- Are you chasing milestones... or building memories?
- Do you believe leadership means going first, or going together?
- Where in your life are you trying to summit alone? What would change if you stopped?
- What connections have you walked past, too focused on the peak to see them?

The mountains teach it. The culture embodies it. The trail insists on it:

We rise when we move together.

Check your mindset. Your summit might not be a place. It might be a person beside youBecause the real victory? Is walking every step with people who matter

MINDSET CHECK
Base Camp Edition

You don't have to be in the Himalayas to do an altitude check on your life.

Take a moment, right now, and answer these honestly:

- Am I mentally training for the life I say I want? Or just hoping it shows up?
- Who are the five people I spend the most time with? Are they climbing, or coasting?
- When discomfort shows up, do I run from it, numb it, or learn from it?
- What is one belief I need to challenge in order to reach my next elevation?
- Would the version of me at 17,599 feet be proud of the choices I'm making today?

Remember: You don't rise to your goals, you fall to your patterns.

If you want higher ground, you need summit-level thinking to get there.

DAY 10
The Descent Begins: Helicopter from Gorak Shep to Lukla

Mindset Shift: From Endurance to Perspective – The real summit is understanding the journey, not just surviving it.

The morning after reaching Everest Base Camp, we woke in Gorak Shep to a stillness that felt almost foreign. No more countdowns. No more altitude gains. Just a quiet ache in our bones, the kind that settles in once the adrenaline fades and the mission is complete.

Outside, the wind was already stirring. The Khumbu Glacier groaned beneath the morning light, and our breath came out in clouds. But something had shifted. Our pace had changed. The push was over. Now came the pull, back toward sea level, back toward life as we'd known it ... only we weren't the same people anymore.

We had planned for this moment: a helicopter flight from Gorak Shep to Lukla. It was a strategic decision, not a shortcut, a conscious choice to avoid the relentless descent that shatters knees and drains spirits. But in the Himalayas, even a plan is just a suggestion.

The morning's flight list was full, and the first seats out were rightfully reserved for those in crisis. One of them was a man from South Charlotte, just a few miles from our own neighborhood, who hadn't taken Diamox and was now in the throes of acute altitude sickness. He was ghostly pale, dehydrated, and unable to keep food or water down. His summit bid was over. All because of a $10 prescription he chose not to take.

Watching him, I felt an ache deeper than altitude. We'd made different choices, but we'd come here chasing something similar, something big enough to risk everything for. And now, here he was, broken by the mountain before he ever reached the top. It was a hard but honest reminder: preparation is not optional up here. Altitude is not impressed by pride. Humility, not ego, is the currency of survival in these places.

My dad and I had taken our Diamox faithfully, paired with a cocktail of Tylenol and Motrin, every day since Kathmandu. Aside from a dehydration headache I earned by skipping my water the night before, trying to avoid a brutal midnight trip to the frozen squat toilet, we'd held up well. That last headache was on me. Tactical error and an important lesson learned.

But the real story of the day wasn't about pills or protocols. It was about the moment we left the ground.

It was our porter Robin's first time in a helicopter. I insisted he take the front seat, a small way to honor the weight he had carried, not just on his back, but in spirit. Just minutes into the flight, the door on his side flew open mid-air.

The cabin filled with chaos, wind roaring in, straps flapping, eyes wide with panic. Robin looked at me. I looked at him. And without thinking, we both leaned forward, grabbed the door, and held it shut together, two sets of hands pressing against the sky. No words. Just instinct.

We were only in the air for ten minutes between Gorak Shep and Pheriche, but those were ten minutes I won't forget. When we landed, Robin turned to me beaming like a child who had just touched the stars. His grin said everything. I was just grateful to be back on solid ground.

The chopper circled back to pick up my dad and Prashant. Then, in a blur of spinning blades, we lifted again, soaring above the path we had bled across. Beneath us unfolded a living map: the switchbacks of Namche, the wide valley of Dingboche, the stark emptiness of Thukla Pass, and the glacial sprawl we had walked beside, wordless and watchful

What had taken nine days of grind, and gasping breath passed beneath us in a matter of minutes. But somehow, seeing it from above didn't diminish it. It made it *bigger*.

Perspective doesn't come from the climb. It comes from looking back. And sometimes, the only way to understand the road is to rise above it.

From the air, it all looked smaller. But the story it told felt even bigger.

We banked over the river valley, the Dudh Kosi flashing like a silver vein cutting through the green. Below us, yaks moved like ants along narrow trails, their loads swaying, their steps sure. Porters in bright jackets wound up steep hillsides, faces turned to the sun, still carrying weight—some visible, some not. Villages that had taken us hours to reach flickered by in seconds: Namche, Monjo, Phakding—each one a mile marker not just of distance, but of growth.

I pressed my forehead to the window, eyes scanning the land that had tested every part of me. What we had climbed up slowly—day by day, heartbeat by breath—we now flew over in minutes. But altitude doesn't erase effort. It just reframes it.

And suddenly, I could see it all again. The exhaustion. The altitude. The silence between steps. I remembered the nights wrapped in down, the sound of yak bells in the dark, the sting of cold water against tired skin. I remembered Dingboche's brutal chill, the sharp thin air of Lobuche, the moment the Khumbu Icefall came into view like a frozen gatekeeper. And I remembered the way the wind carried prayer flags out over impossible drops, like messages whispered across lifetimes.

I looked again at my dad, and this time I didn't see the miles between us—the years, the differences, the weight we'd both carried separately. I saw what remained: two people who had walked the same path, literally and metaphorically. Not to prove anything. But to remember. To reconnect. To return to something essential.

The mountains have a way of stripping everything away—status, certainty, ego—until only the truth is left. And the truth is, we didn't need the summit to feel changed. We didn't need a flag or a photo to know we'd done something that mattered.

We needed the walk. We needed the effort. We needed each other.

As the airstrip at Lukla came into view, clinging to the mountainside like a dare, I felt a surprising stillness inside me. Not relief, exactly. Something else. Like I'd left a piece of myself behind, but also reclaimed something I didn't know was missing.

And as we touched down, the rotors still humming above us, I realized: This journey hadn't taken us to the top of the world. But it had brought us back to the center of ourselves.

Reflection: The summit moment doesn't always happen on the mountain. Sometimes, it happens when you look down and realize what it took to get there, and who you became along the way.

MINDSET CHECK
How Far Do You Have to Rise to Understand the Ground You've Covered?

Mindset Shift: *From Endurance to Perspective — The real summit is understanding the journey, not just surviving it.*

- Are you giving yourself credit for how far you've come, or only measuring progress by how much is left?
- What might shift in your life if you paused to rise above the daily grind and look back at the trail you've walked?
- Where is pride getting in the way of preparation? What's your version of the "$10 decision?"
- Are you holding the door shut with someone metaphorically or literally and missing the power of that shared resilience?
- What moment in your journey deserves a second look not because it was perfect, but because it changed you.

Growth isn't always loud. Sometimes, it looks like wind in your face at 17,000 feet ... and realizing the real summit was never the rocks beneath your boots, it was the clarity rising in your chest.

DAYS 10 TO 12
What If the Hard Part Isn't Over When You Think It Is?

Mindset Shift: From Control to Surrender – Some mountains don't move until you stop pushing.

We landed in Lukla thinking we were finished. The trekking was over. Base Camp had been reached. The mission, at least on paper, was complete. My boots were caked in dust, my legs sore but functional, and my mind was beginning to settle into the idea that we had made it. I had started imagining the clean clothes, the warm showers, the first cup of real coffee in Kathmandu. And beef! I hadn't left Lukla before I told my husband to make burgers the day I got home - I was ready to be off our 11 days of vegetarianism. I was ready to decompress.

But the mountain had one more lesson for us. And it wasn't about climbing, it was about waiting.

Lukla is a strange place to be stranded. It's perched on a knife's edge at 9,383 feet, and the airport, with its famously short and sloped runway, is carved into the side of the mountain like someone ran out of flat land and just said, "Close enough." The airstrip ends in a wall of rock on one end and drops into a deep valley on the other. Every takeoff and landing feels like a stunt.

But the real danger isn't the design, it's the weather. Fog creeps in fast. Clouds roll over the ridgelines without warning. And the moment visibility drops, everything stops. There's no radar to guide planes in and out, no margin for error. If the sky says no, you don't argue.

We were scheduled to fly out the morning after we landed. But when we woke up and stepped outside, the clouds were already swallowing the horizon. The air was damp and heavy, like the mountain was pressing pause. No planes arrived. No planes left. Travelers gathered near the airport with daypacks and the hope that someone, anyone, would call their name. Hours passed. The clouds held.

Day one slipped by in a fog of boiled tea, card games, and quiet pacing.
Day two brought the realization that we weren't in control anymore. Not of the schedule, not of the weather, not of the story we thought we were done writing.

Lukla Airport is cold. Unreasonably cold. Not just outside, but inside too, because *inside* is still just a concrete room with plastic chairs and no insulation. There's no heat. No announcements. You can see your breath as you sit wrapped in down, fingers curled around a scalding hot cup of lemon tea, trying to stay warm and patient at the same time. Everyone's layered up in dirty trek clothes and puffy jackets, some still in the same socks they wore to Base Camp. But no one complains out loud, not yet. Because everyone knows the same truth: you leave when the mountain lets you. Not a moment sooner.

People drift in and out of the terminal, standing near the windows or huddled against walls. Some sit in silence. Others whisper anxiously in small groups, eyes constantly scanning the sky for a break in the clouds. The airstrip itself looks like a dare—a short sliver of asphalt pinned to a cliff. Pilots land here only when visibility is clear and wind is low. And when it's not? You wait.

The tension builds slowly. No one wants to be the first to panic, but it's there—in every deep sigh, every glance toward the clouds, every foot shuffle on the freezing floor. Everyone wants the same thing: Kathmandu. A hot shower. A real bed. A return to softness.

But some travelers are on their own. No guide. Limited English. They sit on their packs, wide-eyed, unsure who to ask or where to go. Confusion flickers across faces as airport staff move briskly from door to door, shouting boarding calls no one seems to understand. The uncertainty is louder than the announcements. And when flights are delayed, or cancelled, no one really explains why. You just wait. Sometimes all day.

And then, occasionally, the silence breaks. A rotor in the distance. A buzz. A glimpse of a chopper or fixed-wing plane cutting through the clouds. Everyone stands. Every head turns. Hearts rise, hoping it's theirs. Sometimes it is. Sometimes it's not.

And the worst part? Nothing else could be done until flights were officially canceled—which could take hours. You'd wait all morning with your boots half-laced and your pack ready, just in case your name got called. But until someone somewhere made the decision to scrub the flight, you were stuck in limbo. Not quite going. Not quite staying. No backup plan. No new itinerary. Just waiting.

In many ways, it reminded me of the military. Hurrying up and waiting. That maddening rhythm where you prepare with urgency, only to stand by for hours with no movement, no answers, and no end in sight. I even joked with my dad—an old phrase my friends and I used to throw around on deployment whenever the boredom started to fray at the edges of our sanity: "Why does nothing keep happening?"

He laughed, because he got it. He'd lived it too.

We sat there, side by side, bundled in everything we owned, watching the same cloud bank roll across the same mountains we'd just walked through. Around us, people fidgeted, whispered, rearranged gear for the third time. Some scrolled endlessly on their phones. Others stared out the windows like they could will the weather to shift. But the mountain didn't care.

That was the lesson again—the same one we kept learning in different forms. You are not in control out here. Not of the sky. Not of the schedule. Not even of your exit.

All you can do is show up, stay ready, and hold on to your sense of humor as long as it lasts.

There's a unique kind of frustration that shows up when you think the hard part is over, when you've already earned your celebration, but the next chapter refuses to begin. You feel entitled to rest, to closure, to motion. And yet, there we were, grounded. No path forward. No real way back.

I kept checking the sky like it owed me something. But it didn't. The mountain never did.

At some point, I realized I was still operating like a climber, trying to push, plan, and problem-solve my way into momentum. But this wasn't a summit. There was nothing to conquer here. Only weather. Only waiting.

That's where the shift happened. That's where the mountain, once again, became the teacher.

Because waiting isn't passive. It's not a weakness. It's not wasted time. It's a different kind of strength, the kind that doesn't get celebrated in highlight reels or summit photos. The kind that requires you to sit still, fully present, and let go of the illusion that you're in charge.

We weren't just delayed. We were being asked to *decompress*. To let the trail settle in our bones. To let the weight of the trail speak in its own way. I had been so focused on finishing strong that I almost missed the invitation to finish *changed*.

Alpine Ramble kept working behind the scenes, and eventually, they found a way out: a private helicopter with Piston Air. The price was steep, over $400 per person, but the desire to move was stronger than the sting to the wallet. When the chopper lifted off, the relief was instant. The feeling of freedom returned as the rotors carved through the air, pulling us away from Lukla's cloud-locked cliffs.

But the lesson wasn't over.

For nearly the entire 50-minute ride back to Kathmandu, there was nothing below us but mountains. No roads. No buildings. No movement. Just valleys folding into each other, rivers snaking through the lowlands, prayer flags flapping on remote ridgelines. But the scale of it, the depth, the vastness, wasn't lost. From above, it all looked softer, like a map someone had sketched by hand. Beautiful. Honest. Humbling.

Then, just as suddenly as the quiet had taken hold, the noise returned. Kathmandu appeared like a memory snapping back into focus. Rooftops. Horns. Dust. Traffic. A thousand lives colliding at once. I wasn't ready for it. I wasn't ready for the contrast.

Because part of me was still up there in the clouds, sitting in the stillness.

That's when it hit me: the descent wasn't over. It wasn't measured in altitude or airspeed, it was measured in awareness. In surrender. In how long it takes your spirit to catch up with your body.

The trek had required endurance. The delay required patience. But this moment of re-entry, required something even deeper: trust.

Not in the weather. Not in the itinerary. In yourself.

To carry the mountain with you, without needing to climb it again.

To bring stillness into the chaos. To keep space for reflection, even when distraction demands attention.

Leadership doesn't end when the mission is over. And the journey doesn't end when the plane lands. Some mountains follow you home. Not to weigh you down, but to remind you who you have become when you finally let go of the need to control the outcome.

Sometimes the strongest thing you can do is stop trying to move forward, and just *be* where you are.

We didn't leave Lukla late. We left right on time.

We just didn't know it yet.

MINDSET CHECK
What If the Hard Part Isn't Over When You Think It Is?

You think it's over.

The trail is behind you. The summit photo is on your phone. You've packed the bags, checked the boxes, and made the calls.

And yet... you're still stuck.

Not physically. Not even visibly. But somewhere deeper, between the ending you expected and the release you never really got.

That's the moment this chapter is about.

In Lukla, we were grounded. The sky shut us down. The clouds rolled in. The runway vanished. We thought we were finished, but the mountain wasn't done with us. Because the final test wasn't physical. It was something quieter. Something slower.

It was surrender.

We weren't being punished. We were being given space, space to listen, to process, to realize that coming down isn't always a clean descent. Sometimes, it's a waiting room where the last lesson finally lands.

That training isn't just physical. It's mental. Emotional. Spiritual. It's how you hold yourself when you can't control the outcome. It's how you wait when you'd rather run.

The hardest part isn't always the climb. Sometimes, it's the stillness that follows, the in-between, where the landscape is still but your inner terrain rearranges.

Ask yourself:

- Where in your life are you mistaking stillness for failure? Are you pushing when you're actually meant to pause?
- What delay or detour are you calling a waste, when it might be the very space you need to decompress and grow?
- What outcome are you still trying to force, even though the weather's telling you to wait?
- Can you let a chapter finish *differently* than you imagined, if it means you finish *transformed*?
- What would it look like to carry the mountain's stillness into the noise you're returning to?

Lukla reminded me that leadership doesn't end at the summit. It shows up in the hold. In the humility to stop pushing. In the strength to wait. In the awareness that some mountains only move when you stop trying to move them.

Check your mindset. Sometimes the bravest thing you can do is stand still. And trust that who you're becoming is worth the delay.

DAY 12 TO 14
Return to Kathmandu: Reentry and Reflection

Mindset Shift: From Peak to Perspective – What you carry back is more important than what you leave behind.

After days in the clouds and cold, the moment our helicopter touched down in Kathmandu was almost surreal. The city welcomed us with its familiar chaos, honking horns, the aroma of street food, and the hum of life at full volume. But we had changed.

The noise didn't feel the same.

There's something disorienting about reentry after a high-altitude experience; physical, emotional, and spiritual. You've just spent nearly two weeks in one of the world's most remote and rugged places, with only your breath, your footsteps, and your people. Then suddenly, you're back in a city where everything moves fast and nothing waits.

That transition was harder than I expected.

We checked into our hotel, grateful for clean sheets, hot showers, and strong Wi-Fi. But the stillness of the mountains had changed what we valued. The comforts were appreciated, but they weren't what we were seeking anymore.

Dad and I spent our final days in Kathmandu slowly. We wandered the streets. Ate warm meals. Visited shops and bought my mom, husband, and kids trinkets. But mostly, we processed. There was no rush. No agenda. Just space to reflect.

We talked about the trek, of course, the milestones, the altitude, the aching knees, but we also talked about things that don't often come up in everyday life. Legacy. Regret. Pride. Healing. The mountain had made space for those conversations. Kathmandu let us carry them forward.

There was a quiet satisfaction in knowing we had finished something hard. Together. Without fanfare, but full of meaning.

Completion isn't marked by applause. It's marked by clarity. And clarity doesn't come at the summit. It comes after. In the stillness. In the return.

On our last evening, we sat at a rooftop café and watched the sun set over the city. The smog blushed gold in the fading light. And for the first time, I allowed myself to think about going home.

Not just physically. But mentally. Emotionally. What kind of leader I wanted to be? What kind of parent? What kind of daughter? What kind of person?

This journey had started with a goal: Trek to the Everest Base Camp.

But the real destination was always something quieter.

A return to self.

A reunion with meaning.

A reconnection to what really matters.

Leadership after the mountain means carrying its lessons into the world that forgot them. It means listening more. Speaking with intention. And remembering that every summit demands a return. How you come back matters.

MINDSET CHECK
What If the Stillness Is the Final Test?

There's a moment after the mission, when the trek is done, the summit behind you, and the adrenaline finally wears off, where you think it's time to celebrate. Time to move on. Time to fly home.

But the mountain doesn't let you go that easily.

You find yourself grounded. Waiting. Watching clouds roll in, not just across the runway, but across your mind. You can't push forward. You can't go back. You're stuck in the stillness, in the space between what *was* and what's *next*.

The delay in Lukla wasn't just a scheduling hiccup. It was the final lesson. One that had nothing to do with altitude, and everything to do with surrender. We thought we were finished, but the truth is, we hadn't even begun to *come down*. We were still gripping the timeline, still trying to control the ending. But some chapters don't close on command. Some growth only arrives when you stop forcing the page to turn.

Because here's the truth:

You don't get to control the clouds. You only get to choose who you are while you wait for them to clear.

Ask yourself:

- Where in your life are you trying to fly home before the lesson has landed?

- When have you mistaken stillness for weakness, when it was actually wisdom?
- What would it look like to stop pushing and start trusting?
- Are you so focused on what's next that you're missing who you're becoming *right now*?
- What might change if you saw your delay as an invitation, not an interruption?

Lukla reminded me that leadership isn't just about momentum, it's about composure in the pause. Patience in the unknown. Grace in the grip.

Check your mindset. The mission might be over, but the mountain is still speaking.
Can you be quiet enough to hear it?

Final Chapter

Final Chapter

ONE STEP, ONE MISSION

Mindset Shift: From Parallel Paths to Shared Legacy – The summit isn't the end. It's the moment you understand who walked beside you.

By the time we reached Base Camp, the altitude wasn't the hardest part. The climb had become something more; a mirror. Each step upward reflected a deeper truth: the way we've led, the way we've loved, the way we've carried others along the way.

My father and I had spent decades on parallel paths. Both Soldiers. Both leaders. But we never truly walked side by side, until this mountain.

On the trail, we leaned into each other's strengths. When my breath ran short and my legs faltered, I looked to him, steady, deliberate, still moving forward. He's spent a lifetime in service. Decades of deployments. Years overseas. But what's more impressive is what hasn't changed: his purpose, his presence, his quiet discipline.

He'd never label it resilience. He doesn't have to. He just lives it.

Our most meaningful moments weren't on the summits. They were in the quiet, inside tea houses, wrapped in blankets while the wind howled outside. We shared stories over honey lemon ginger tea and wooden tables. We laughed with fellow trekkers. We swapped war stories with a former Australian Infantryman who immediately understood us, because veterans don't need icebreakers. We already speak the language.

I watched my dad come alive in those conversations. I've heard many of his stories before, but I never get tired of them. His dry humor. His way of underselling chaos. His clarity under pressure. He doesn't perform. He remembers.

And as I listened, I realized something I hadn't before.

We both led with heart. Just differently.

He's the quiet professional, calm, strategic, steady. He never yelled. He never needed to. He took care of his people through the system, through precision and policy.

I was the Officer of the People; present, emotional, relational. I built trust, asked questions, and walked with my Soldiers through their highs and lows. I invested in them the way I wanted someone to invest in me.

Two styles. One shared mission: take care of your people.

That's what the mountain gave me, not just a physical achievement, but the clarity to see my father fully. Not just as the man who raised me. But as a leader, I respect. A mentor I admire. A teammate I'm proud to walk beside.

Reflection: The mountain didn't give me anything new. It gave me back something I'd carried all along, a deeper understanding of who my father is, and the legacy we're still writing. One quiet step at a time.

Post Script: The Echo of Everest

I didn't come home with a summit photo. There's no shot of me on top of Everest, arms raised in triumph. No flags. No crowds. No records broken.

But I didn't need one.

What I brought home was something far less visible, and far more enduring. I brought home stillness. Perspective. Proof. Not proof of strength, but of resilience. Not proof of skill, but of presence. Proof that I could be broken open by something far greater than myself... and choose to keep walking anyway.

We traveled nearly forty miles through some of the most breathtaking and brutal terrain on Earth. But this story was never about distance. It was about what we carried ... and what we left behind.

I didn't just walk to Everest Base Camp, I walked through years of noise, self-doubt, and questions I hadn't dared to answer. And I walked beside the man who taught me what it means to serve, to lead, and to endure. My father didn't have to say much on that trail. He didn't need to. His presence said everything.

There were moments the mountain stripped us bare, not just physically, but emotionally. Moments when all we could do was breathe. Moments when we couldn't catch our breath at all. We struggled to sleep. We struggled to eat. We even struggled to use the bathroom. But we showed up. Every day. Every step. And I learned that is what real leadership looks like.

It's not about being the strongest in the room. It's not about having all the answers. It's about presence. Grit. Service. It's about believing in yourself enough to keep going, even when it's hard, even when you're tired, even when the summit is nowhere in sight.

Since returning, people have asked me what this trek taught me. Some days, I talk about the way the wind speaks when nothing else does, high above the treeline. Or the impossible blues of the sky. Or the moment I cried in the middle of the trail, windburned cheeks and sunglasses hiding everything but the truth. Other days, I talk about Snickers bars, yak dung fires, and my dad's ridiculous joy at knowing a helicopter was coming to get us.

But if I had to give just one answer?

This trek taught me to remember who I am. Not the version on the résumé. Not the one in the uniform. Not the curated one with titles or filters. The version who walks. Who breaks. Who breathes. Who believes. Who keeps going. That's who I am.

And for whatever it's worth, if you're reading this and you've ever felt lost, disconnected, or unsure if you still have what it takes … I'm here to tell you: You do.

I hope you find your own Everest. It doesn't have to look like mine. It just has to be hard enough to humble you and holy enough to change you. Keep walking. And take someone with you when you do. Because at the end of it all, the view was spectacular. But the company? That was the best part.

Two weeks after I returned from Nepal, my husband, Michael, attended Squad Up Summit, a real estate investment conference hosted by Subto and Pace Morby. In a single weekend, he sat in the presence of giants. Dr. Jordan Peterson challenged attendees to take ownership of their identity and legacy. Codie Sanchez peeled back the layers on building freedom through cash-flowing, contrarian businesses.

David Goggins cracked open the raw truth of what it takes to push through pain and limitation. Dean Graziosi broke down the power of mindset and abundance. And Justin Tuminowski, a New England investor deeply rooted in service, spoke with clarity and purpose that resonated with him on a personal level. Michael connected with another investor, Mike Jackson, who I'd joked that I would make money with one day prior to Michael leaving for Squad Up Summit. Mike Jackson and I, as of this book being published, partnered together to assist Agents on low equity Subject to real estate deals.

But one voice brought everything full circle: Stacy Allison, the first American woman to summit Mount Everest. She didn't stand on the summit the first time she tried. She failed. And she had to return. To regroup. To recommit. Her dream didn't come easily, but she never let that first failure define her. And when she did reach the top, she said something that will stay with me forever:

"You don't conquer Everest. You collaborate with it."

That hit deep. Because I'd lived it just on the way to Base Camp. The truth is, you don't conquer life either. You don't summit big dreams alone. Every great thing we achieve is built in collaboration. With teammates. With mentors. With family. .

Sitting in that room, surrounded by people who had climbed their own Everests and in Stacy's case, literally stood at the summit, lit a fire in Michael. At that moment, I realized my three-week journey to the summit of Mount Everest had changed both Michael and me.

As I write this, Michael and I are working with a growing team of real estate investors, nonprofits, Veteran advocates, and local and federal agencies working to solve the affordable housing crisis across the United States. Our first stop? Charlotte, NC. Our first priority is Veterans. The very people who have served this country with courage, and who now deserve stable, dignified housing in return.

We're bringing together every thread of our journey: service, grit, collaboration, and belief. We're not waiting for permission. We're building what's needed, brick by brick, relationship by relationship.

At one point, I thought the trek to Everest Base Camp was my Everest. But what it gave me was clarity. Conviction. Courage.

Simon Sinek talks about "finding your why." And this? This is mine.

My purpose has always been service. Now I have the voice, the vision, the team, and the unshakable belief in myself to go make change where it's needed most.

The Khumbu Valley didn't just teach me to keep going. It reminded me: I was never lost. I was just being shaped for something bigger.

And now?

Now, I climb for others.

FROM A FATHER'S EYES

By Tim Platt

A fter a year of preparation, pouring over packing lists, training hikes on local trails, and watching enough Everest Base Camp YouTube videos to last a lifetime, I found myself standing beside my daughter Rachel, 17,599 feet above sea level, at the foot of the world's tallest mountain.

It was 2:45 PM on March 10, 2025.

I was 67 years old. Rachel was 41. And there we were, two generations, side by side, having reached Everest Base Camp together. We had made it.

But our journey wasn't just about altitude or geography. It was about endurance. Resilience. And love.

Along the way, we were joined by two remarkable young men, our guide, Pershant (27), and our porter, Robin (17), who became more than companions. They became part of our team, our rhythm, our shared heartbeat on the trail.

What surprised me most, though, was how the mountain stripped away everything except what mattered most. Every step, every breath, every moment forced us to slow down, to listen to ourselves, to each other, and to the stillness that connected us. It tested us in ways we couldn't have predicted. Not just physically, but emotionally.

On day two, we hit what we now jokingly call our "train wreck" moment. Nothing was going right. Our pace was off, our bodies weren't adjusting, and the dream felt like it was slipping through our fingers. But something happened at that low point. We adapted. We leaned on each other. We reminded ourselves that we were stronger together.

And from that point on, we moved differently, not just on the trail, but in our relationship. We weren't just father and daughter. We were teammates. We were co-adventurers. We were walking toward something bigger than a mountain.

Standing at Base Camp, I didn't feel victorious. I felt grateful. For the mountain. For the challenge. And most of all, for the time with my daughter that I will never forget.

We climbed together. We struggled together. And in the process, we became closer than we'd ever been.

That, to me, was the real summit.

Reading Group Guide: Everest Base Camp Memoir

Themes to Explore

- Transition and transformation
- Leadership in and out of uniform
- Parent-child dynamics
- Purpose after service
- Resilience, endurance, and identity
- Spirituality, silence, and personal growth
- What it means to come "home"

Discussion Questions

Trek as Metaphor

1. The trek to Everest Base Camp is a literal journey, but it also symbolizes deeper transitions. What "mountains" did the author carry into the Himalayas? What do you think she left behind?
2. Which moment in the trek (emotional, physical, or spiritual)resonated most with you? Why?

Veterans & Identity

3. The book explores what happens when the mission ends. What parallels did you see between transitioning out of the military and reentering civilian life?
4. How does the author confront or redefine her sense of value and identity post-service?
5. In what ways can civilians better support or understand veterans in transition?

Leadership & Service

6. How does the memoir challenge conventional definitions of leadership? What moments stood out as examples of "quiet leadership"?
7. Think about the guides, porters, and Sherpa community in the story. How do they model servant leadership? What lessons can Western leaders take from their approach?
8. What does the author's relationship with her father reveal about generational leadership and how it evolves over time?

Reflection & Connection

9. The author writes: *"Leadership after the mountain means carrying its lessons into the world that forgot them."* What does that mean to you? How do we hold onto lessons from pivotal moments in our lives?
10. What role does silence, stillness, or spiritual reflection play in the book? How might these practices help people after trauma, loss, or transition?

Application

11. What is *your* Everest? Is there a journey (physical, emotional, or otherwise) that you've been avoiding? What's one step you could take toward it?
12. How did this book make you think differently about family, healing, or purpose?

Group Activities

- Create your own "Mindset Shift" from the past year, something you've learned, and how it's changed you.
- Write a short letter to your past or future self, reflecting on your own journey.
- Identify a "porter" in your life, someone who has carried unseen weight for others, and discuss how to recognize and honor that support.

BASE CAMP LEADERSHIP – A MOUNTAIN ACRONYM

Leadership isn't a title. It's not the loudest voice in the room or the sharpest strategy on paper. I didn't truly understand that until I was out of the boardroom and into the thin air above 17,000 feet, placing one deliberate foot in front of the other toward Everest Base Camp. There's no posturing on the trail, no hiding behind buzzwords or bravado. Out here, leadership strips down to what's real. What's lived.

Out here, *you either lead with intention or you fall behind.*

Each step on the trail revealed something different. A test. A truth. A reminder of what it means to guide, serve, and endure. Somewhere between Namche Bazaar and the Khumbu Glacier, I started shaping a new leadership framework, one that didn't come from a seminar or a whitepaper, but from the cold, hush of the Himalayas. I call it **BASE CAMP Leadership**. And like the mountain, it doesn't let you fake it.

B – Balance

The mountain demands it. Push too hard, and it humbles you. Move too slowly, and you lose momentum. I learned to balance drive with rest, confidence with humility. As a leader, it's easy to tip toward hustle culture, to think that more grind equals more growth. But out here, I realized that *real strength is in knowing when to pause*. When to breathe. When to look back and ensure your team is still with you. Balance isn't weakness. It's wisdom.

A – Adaptability

Plans are good until the weather changes. Until altitude hits. Until the route shifts or someone gets sick, or you realize your assumptions were wrong. Adaptability on the trail meant listening to our guides, adjusting pace, even calling audibles when our bodies spoke louder than our egos. In leadership, it's the same. The strongest leaders aren't rigid, they pivot with purpose. They respond to change without losing their core direction.

S – Service

This one hit hardest. I watched our guides, Dil and Prashant, carry gear, check oxygen levels, offer encouragement, and always with a calm, quiet grace. No fanfare. No selfies. Just service. Back home, I'd read about servant leadership, but here I *felt it*. Leadership isn't about being followed. It's about *lifting others, even when no one's watching*. Even when you're exhausted. Especially then.

E – Endurance

We didn't climb Everest, but make no mistake, getting to Base Camp was a grind. Your lungs burn. Your legs ache. You question your decision to be there. And that's when it hits you: endurance isn't about pushing through pain. It's about showing up anyway. It's about embracing the suck, honoring the moment, and *choosing to keep going when quitting would be easier*. In business, in life, in leadership, it's grit over glory.

C – Compassion

For others, yes. But also for yourself. There was a moment in Dingboche where I watched clouds wrap around Ama Dablam like a silk scarf. The stillness was unreal. And I realized: I had been hard on myself for so long. Measuring worth by achievement. That day, I gave myself grace. As a leader, if you don't lead with compassion, your team will burn out, and so will you. Start with yourself. Then extend it outward.

A – Accountability

The trail doesn't let you hide. You either did your acclimatization hike or you didn't. You either packed your gear, or you deal with the cold. In life, it's the same. Leaders are accountable not just to KPIs or project deadlines, but to people. To values. To those quiet promises we make to ourselves in the mirror. *Are you living what you say you believe?*

M – Mindset

Altitude sickness starts in the body, but it grows in the mind. I had to train my thoughts, not just my legs. I had to catch myself in spirals of doubt and redirect with purpose. *Mindset isn't fluff, it's the internal compass that guides every decision.* Resilient leaders don't just manage tasks, they master thought patterns. They choose the story they tell themselves and their team.

P – Presence

We stopped often. Not just to rest, but to look. To take in the impossible blues of the glacier lakes, the wild jagged skyline of the Himalayas, and the prayer flags whipping in the wind. I learned to stop racing toward the summit and *be where my boots were.* In leadership, presence is everything. Listening fully. Seeing people. *Leadership doesn't always mean going first, sometimes it means going together.*

The mountain didn't make me a leader. It just *revealed* the one I want to be. Someone grounded in service, anchored in mindset, and driven by something deeper than accolades or applause.

BASE CAMP Leadership isn't just a framework. It's a compass. One I'll keep using as I climb the next set of mountains, literal or not.

Because in the end, leadership is a lot like trekking: it's lived, one step at a time.

GEAR & PACKING LIST FOR EVEREST BASE CAMP (SHOULDER SEASON)

This packing list is designed for the Spring shoulder season (February to mid-March), when temps drop fast, trails are quieter, and preparation matters most. Everything on this list was tested and trekked by us.

Clothing: Layer Like Your Life Depends on It

- 2x short-sleeve trekking shirts (synthetic or merino)
- 2x long-sleeve base layers (lightweight, breathable)
- 2x thermal base layer tops (midweight to heavyweight)
- 2x thermal bottoms for sleeping or layering
- 1x fleece jacket (Sherpa brand from Namche,10/10 recommend)
- 1x insulated down jacket (packable, water-resistant; we used Paka brand which is a sustainable technical gear

company based out of Peru, they specialize in alpaca fur products)
- 1x hard-shell rain jacket and pants (wet weather protection)
- 2x trekking pants (quick-dry)
- 1x insulated pants for tea house evenings
- 2–3x moisture-wicking T-shirts
- 1x hoodie or soft fleece for comfort
- 5–7x moisture-wicking underwear
- 2–3x sports bras (for women)
- 1x comfortable sleepwear (you'll thank yourself)
- 1x lightweight gloves (liner)
- 1x insulated/waterproof gloves or mittens
- 1x beanie
- 2x Buffs or neck gaiters (they're lifesavers)
- 1x sun hat or baseball cap
- 1x balaclava (optional,but great for wind)

Footwear: Break. Them. In.

- 1x pair waterproof trekking boots (broken in!)
- 2–3x pairs wool or synthetic hiking socks
- 1x pair thick mountaineering socks (for high altitudes)
- 1x pair camp shower shoes (Crocs or slides = winning)
- 1x pair teahouse shoes (we used Merrill Hut Mocs, that zippered together; a double win because they were light and warm)
- Lightweight gaiters (optional)
- Crampons (optional) – we rented ours and never ended up using them

Gear & Accessories: Your Mobile Home

- 1x daypack (25–35L with waist strap)
- 1x duffel bag (60–80L; porter-carried) – this was provided by our guiding service
- 1x rain cover for daypack
- Trekking poles (essential for knees and river crossings) – we rented these from our guiding service
- Sleeping bag (-10°C or lower rating)
- Sleeping bag liner (-30°C if you run cold)
- Headlamp + extra batteries
- Sunglasses (UV protection)
- 2x water bottles (including 1L wide-mouth Nalgene for hot water)
- 1 x Nalgene insulator sleeve (this comes in clutch when the weather dips below freezing; warm water is far easier to drink than freezing water)
- Water purification method (Steripen, filter, or tablets) – I recommend getting these from your home country in order to ensure 1) effectiveness and 2) taste. Everything I'd read showed that the tablets in Nepal had a bitter taste.

Toiletries & Hygiene: Stay (Somewhat) Human

- Toothbrush, toothpaste, floss
- Biodegradable soap or shampoo
- Sunscreen (SPF 50+)
- Lip balm with SPF (your lips will thank you)

- Quick-dry towel
- Baby/body wipes (lavender-scented for morale boosts)
- Toilet paper + hand sanitizer
- Nail clippers, comb, hair ties
- Ear plugs + eye mask (tea house essentials)
- Feminine hygiene products (as needed)

Medical & First Aid: Pack for Prevention

- Prescription medications (including Diamox)
- Electrolyte tablets or powders (key at altitude)
- Ibuprofen / Tylenol / cold meds
- Imodium or anti-diarrheal
- Blister pads
- Antibiotic ointment
- Pulse oximeter (optional but helpful)

Electronics: Stay Powered Up

- Smartphone + charger
- Smartwatch + charger
- Power bank (minimum 20,000 mAh, 50,000 if sharing)
- Universal travel adapter
- Kindle or paperback book
- Headphones/earbuds
- Camera + extra batteries (optional)

Documents & Misc.

- Passport + 4 passport photos
- Copies of key documents (passport, visa, insurance)
- Travel insurance with high-altitude coverage

- Dry bags or Ziplocks (keep gear dry and sorted) – these can also be purchased on the cheap on Thamel Street when you get to Kathmandu
- Notebook + pen (journal the trek!)
- Small folder for your trek completion certificate
- Packable tote bag (for dirty clothes or souvenirs)

Pro Tip:

At altitude, every ounce counts. But comfort counts too. Choose items that serve multiple purposes, test everything in advance, and don't forget the Buff. Seriously, bring at least two.

TREKKING WITH ALPINE RAMBLE
– A TRUSTED PARTNER ON THE TRAIL

We chose to trek with Alpine Ramble Treks, a guiding company based in Kathmandu, Nepal, and it was one of the best decisions of the entire journey. From start to finish, Alpine Ramble offered expert guidance, exceptional hospitality, and a true sense of community.

Why We Chose Them

- Outstanding reviews and reputation for safety
- All-inclusive pricing and transparency
- Focus on small group experiences and personalized service
- Local knowledge and support of the Sherpa community

Cost: $1,255 per person (as of 2025)

What's Included:

- Round-trip domestic flights (Kathmandu to Lukla)
- Airport pick-up and drop-off
- Licensed guide and porter (including meals, lodging, and insurance)
- 3 meals per day on the trail
- Lodging in tea houses throughout the trek
- Trekking permits and TIMS card
- Welcome dinner and farewell dinner in Kathmandu
- Trek completion certificate and commemorative gifts
- Daily oxygen saturation and heart rate checks
- Sleeping bag and down jacket upon request
- Trail snacks: Snickers, cookies, fruit
- Emergency evacuation coordination (covered by your own insurance)

What's Not Included:

- International airfare
- Nepal entry visa ($50 USD for 30 days)
- Travel insurance (must cover high-altitude trekking)
- Beverages (tea, bottled water, soda, etc.)
- Charging fees or Wi-Fi access at tea houses
- Room upgrades (we paid $65 per day for electric blankets and private baths)
- Porter tips and guide gratuities (expected and appreciated)
- Additional meals in Kathmandu before or after the trek

People Who Made It Memorable

We would be remiss if we didn't give a heartfelt thank you to the incredible team that made this journey unforgettable:

- **Gil** – CEO and founder of Alpine Ramble. His commitment to ethical trekking and empowering local guides made us feel like we were part of something meaningful. Communication before and after the trek was seamless. He's built the business from the ground up having been a porter, a trekking guide and summited to Camp 2 of Everest.
- **Prashant** – Our lead guide. Professional, warm, funny, and deeply knowledgeable. His calm leadership and cultural wisdom were invaluable. He will always remain the "Boss of the Mountains," to my father and I.
- **Robin** – Our porter. Only 17 years old and strong as an ox. He carried our gear with humility and heart. This trip also gave Robin his first helicopter ride, and we were honored to share it with him.

We recommend requesting these three by name if you plan your own Everest Base Camp trek. They're the real deal.

Final Reflection: *A good guide gets you to your destination. A great one helps you transform along the way. Alpine Ramble did both.*

BOOKS ABOUT EVEREST
(ADVENTURE, CULTURE & FIRSTHAND ACCOUNTS)

1. Into Thin Air by *Jon Krakauer*
   A gripping, first-person account of the 1996 Everest disaster,equal parts memoir, thriller, and cautionary tale.
2. Touching My Father's Soul by *Jamling Tenzing Norgay*
   A deeply personal and spiritual look at Everest, written by the son of one of its first summiteers.
3. *Everest, Inc.: The Renegades and Rogues Who Built an Industry at the Top of the World* explores the rise of Everest as a commercial enterprise, revealing the adventurers, opportunists, and power players who turned the world's highest peak into a high-stakes business..
4. Trekking in the Everest Region by *Jamie McGuinness*
   A practical and historical guidebook that also tells the story of the rise of the trekking industry in the Khumbu region. Great insight into villages, culture, and trails.

5. Everest: Mountain Without Mercy by *Broughton Coburn*
    Stunning National Geographic photography alongside
    stories from climbers and Sherpas alike.

Books on Leadership, Purpose & Self-Discovery

6. Start with Why by *Simon Sinek*
    A must-read on how clarity of purpose creates deeper
    motivation, resilience, and direction in life and work.
7. 12 Rules for Life: An Antidote to Chaos by *Jordan B. Peterson*
    A blend of philosophy, psychology, and practical life
    advice. Grounding, especially for those navigating
    change or challenge.
8. Millionaire Success Habits by *Dean Graziosi*
    Accessible, motivating insights on mindset, habit
    formation, and building a life of impact and
    intentionality.
9. The Obstacle Is the Way by *Ryan Holiday*
    Ancient Stoic principles repackaged for the modern
    world, how to turn trials into triumphs.
10. Atomic Habits by *James Clear*
    Simple, powerful tools for building habits that stick,
    especially useful when prepping physically and mentally
    for a trek like EBC.

Books for Reflection, Stillness & Emotional Growth

11. Man's Search for Meaning by *Viktor E. Frankl*
    A powerful meditation on suffering, survival, and finding
    purpose in even the harshest conditions.

12. The Comfort Crisis by *Michael Easter*
    Argues for the value of choosing hard things,and why doing so can lead to greater happiness, fulfillment, and growth.
13. When Things Fall Apart by *Pema Chödrön*
    Buddhist wisdom for embracing discomfort, letting go of control, and growing through pain.
14. Meditations by *Marcus Aurelius*
    The journal of a Roman emperor, surprisingly relevant today. Ideal reading for the quiet, reflective moments on the trail.

Appendix E

IMAGES

LTC (Ret) Tim Platt pins Airborne wings on his
daughter Rachel during their time serving together on active
duty (2008–2011)—a generational passing of legacy, courage,
and commitment to something greater than self.

Prashant, Tim Platt, Rachel, and Gil on the eve of their Everest Base Camp trek—standing at the threshold of adventure, bonded by anticipation, purpose, and the promise of the path ahead.

A view of Kathmandu from the left side of a Sita Air flight—
where the sprawl of the city fades into the haze, and the jagged
silhouette of the Himalayas begins to rise in the distance.

A plane lifts off from Lukla Airport, leaving behind the world
below. With its steep runway and unpredictable weather, every
takeoff from this mountain perch feels like a leap of faith into
the unknown.

Rachel and Tim standing at the gate marking the start of their Everest Base Camp trek—Day One from Lukla to Phakding.

Rachel, Tim Platt, and their guide Prashant crossing the Hillary Step Bridge—a symbolic turning point on the Everest Base Camp trail where the journey shifts from endurance to transformation.

Prashant, Robin, Tim, and Rachel at Everest View Hotel, with Mount Everest and Ama Dablam towering in the distance—a moment of awe, camaraderie, and shared purpose high above the Khumbu Valley.

A striking sculpture made of collected trash on the trail back to
Namche—an artistic reminder of the environmental impact
even the most remote adventures can leave behind.

A view of Namche Bazaar, the gateway to Everest—nestled into the hillside at 11,300 feet, this vibrant Sherpa village is the last major stop before the real ascent begins.

Rachel making her way back from Everest View Hotel, fighting through the effects of altitude and fatigue. A tough day on the trail that tested both body and mindset.

Rachel and Tim walking the Everest Base Camp trail with
Ama Dablam rising in the background—a quiet stretch of trail
framed by one of the Himalayas' most iconic peaks.

The front of the Dingboche Monastery—a peaceful landmark on the Everest trail that reflects the deep spiritual roots of Tibetan Buddhism in the Khumbu region. A place of prayer, reflection, and blessing for those making the long ascent.

Rachel warming up beside a yak dung stove—an essential source of heat in the high-altitude teahouses of the Khumbu, where comfort is simple, and every bit of warmth is earned.

A team of yaks making their way along the Everest trail—vital to Sherpa culture, these resilient animals carry supplies, food, and gear across rugged terrain, powering life and livelihood in the Himalayas.

Prashant dancing in the clouds, singing "Resham Firiri" with Ama Dablam peeking through the mist behind him—a moment of pure joy and cultural connection high in the Himalayas.

Robin and Prashant on the trail, with Robin wearing the traditional Nepali head strap, or *namlo*, used to porter gear. Many porters, like Robin, train to become guides—an important tradition in the trekking world. As their guide, Prashant sees it as part of his job to grow Robin's skills and confidence for the path ahead.

A mani stone memorial at Thukla Pass, where dozens of
tributes honor climbers who lost their lives on Everest. Set high
above the Khumbu Valley, this somber stretch of trail offers a
powerful pause—a sacred place to reflect on ambition, loss,
and the unforgiving majesty of the mountain.

Prashant, Robin, Tim, and Rachel at Everest Base Camp—tired, grateful, and standing at 17,598 feet, united by every step, story, and struggle that brought them to the base of the world's highest peak.

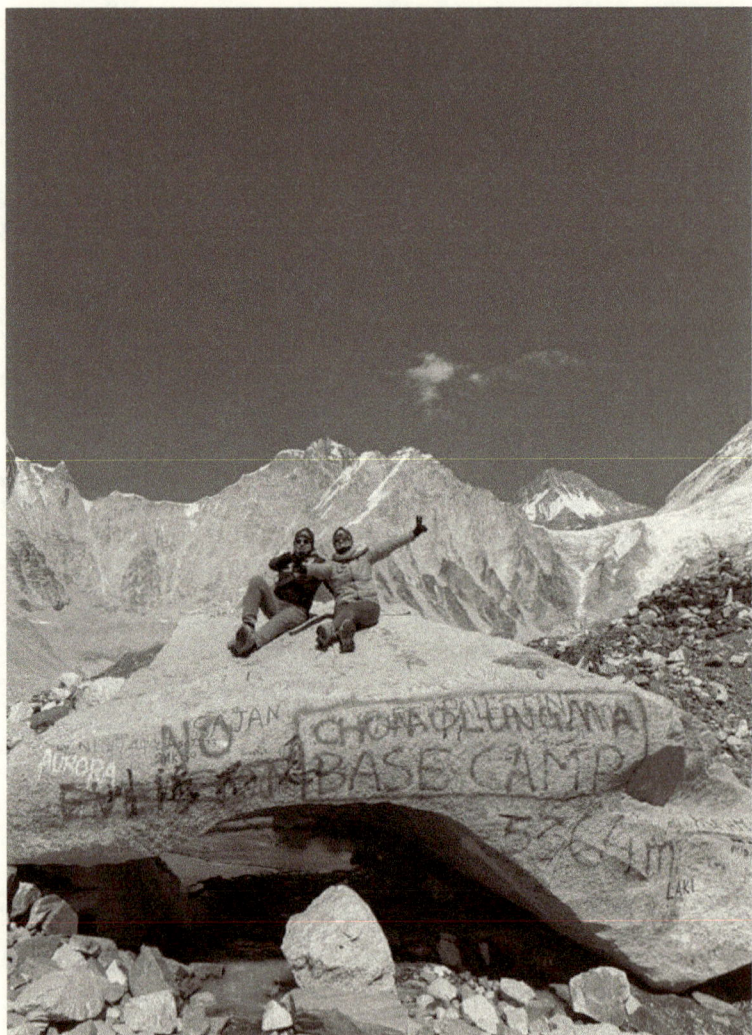

Tim and Rachel on the Everest Base Camp rock—marking the end of a 40-mile journey and the culmination of a shared dream, carved into stone at the foot of the world's highest mountain.

A view of Gorak Shep, the last outpost before Everest Base
Camp, with the towering peak of Mount Everest rising in the
background—a stark, beautiful reminder of how close and how
humbling the final stretch can be.